THE VIEW
FROM
SUNNYBANK

Dee Blair

Printed by CreateSpace 2010

ISBN: 1449905978
EAN-13: 9781449905972

Printed in the United States of America

DEDICATION

For my husband, Joe, and for my faithful readers,

who have waited a long time for this book.

TABLE OF CONTENTS

Dedication	iii
Table of Contents	iv
Preface	viii
Fowl Deeds Done in Dead of Night	1
A Magnificent, Bird-Brained Obsession	4
Laughter—Often the Best Medicine	7
The Wonderful Rebirth of Three Lives	9
Alien Thoughts in a Foreign Garden	12
Masked Bandits and Peeping Toms	15
Train of Thought	18
Freezertown	21
An Airborne Visitation	24
Winter Meditations	27
Requiem for a Fruit Fly	29
Chaos at Caribou Coffee	31
Dive! Dive! Robin Attacks a Hood!	33
A Titanic Challenge for Nobody Special	36
"Memories...light the corners of my mind..."	39
Yarns and Small Tails	42
On the Very Edge of Flight	45
The Garden, a Lady, a Life Remembered	48
Crotchety Crank, Hammocky Howls	51
Stunning Vistas, Gargoyle Thoughts	54
From Terror to Triumph: A Man and His Music	57

A Swinging Hotel for Feline Phantoms   60
Poetry in Motion: Toronto Horse Magic   63
Stealthy Home Invaders   66
An Unforgettable Cat Tale   69
An Alley Explorer's Adventure   72
A 2008 Makeover: Tweaking Me   75
Beetles, Lice and Long Memories   78
Canine Wish: "Let It Rain! Let It Pour!"   81
More On Sailor, An Old Seadog   84
Uh-Oh! Foot-Draggers Stalk Grand Opera   86
More Opera Shenanigans   89
My Iron Cinderella—Beauty in Chains   91
Spooky Machine Machinations   94
Machine Gripes—A Final Rant   97
Little Disasters That Cheer Up God   100
Knotty Thoughts: A Door Soliloquy   103
All Things Wise and Wonderful   106
Armchair Adventures and Spring Ghosts   109
Wishy-Washy brooms vs. Brooms   112
Talkin' Trash: A Scavenger's Tale   115
Ducks Consider Gardener a Quack   118
Falling in Love with Trashed Toenails   121
Nanny Trees Stump Bully, Lend Support   124
Bowser's Beastly Adventure   127
Alley Adventure Still Haunts Bowser   130

"Flowered" Elk Lake Memories   132
A Pork-Pie Hat's Blustery Adventure   135
Duckling Delights, Mama's Mistake   137
All That Glitters: A Padlock's Tour   140
Eavesdropping On Teen Talk   143
A Gremlin Plague   146
When Two Worlds Gently Bump   149
Wormy Halloween Thoughts   152
Odd Duck, Mish-Mash Thoughts   155
Unwashed, Unschooled, Unrivaled Genius   158
Flakes, Felines, and Field Mice   161
The Glums, Mr. Grinch, and Simple Gifts   164
Odd Birds   167
Snowed Rodents and White Art   170
Magic Fingers, Marvelous Evening   173
Lilliputian View of an Alien World   176
Bandits, Bees and Copycats   179
Two Kinds of Slime, and One Diamond   182
Our Bray-zen Paddy MacDonk   185
Encounters in a Parallel Dimension   188
Washed-Out English Thoughts   191
An English Teashop Reminiscence   194
English Backbone   197
A Feast of Words and Their Tweaks   199
The White Invader Sleighs England   202

Death's Nose Tweaked Twice	205
Sketches of Alien Lives	207
Soggy, Delicious Memories	210
Oops! Bonked-Brain Bloopers Bemuse	213
British English Baffles Bumpkin	216
Missing Thoughts, and Miss Charlotte	219
Storm Over Aberystwyth	222
TV Thump-Thump Woes—and Excesses	225
Kate: How She Saved Her Own Life	228
A Mothering Sunday Rescue	231
Bangs, Bruises, and Blink-Outs	234
Ancient Chester—Moans and Marvels	237
Two Disasters That Didn't Happen	241
Resurrection of the Almost-Dead	244
Senior Moments, Quacks, and The Donald	247
Diligent Dilbert Delivers: Part One	250
Diligent Dilbert Delivers: Part Two	253
It's a Wonderful Life!	256
A Fair Day in Herefordshire	259
Another Dumb Bunny Bummer	262
A Car-Chosen, Timeless Tour	265
Bumping Heads with British Bankers	268
Battling a Slow-Motion Monster	271
The Beginning of the End	274
Home is Where the Heart Is	277

PREFACE

I love words. My family has long noticed my delight in creating a good turn of phrase; this knack runs in the family, as my mother wrote a brilliant autobiography before she passed away, and my two daughters have published poetry and nonfiction for many years. But I came late to publishing, myself.

In 1991, my husband Joe and I purchased a Queen Anne home on historic Sixth Street in Traverse City, Michigan. I named it Sunnybank, partly because Sixth Street runs along the banks of the Boardman River, and partly after the house in Albert Payson Terhune's wonderful book *Lad: A Dog*. After restoring the house to my liking, I looked around the property and asked myself, "What's next?" The garden, of course. I hadn't a clue about how to grow things back then. So I learned by reading—and by doing. From humble beginnings, the back yard gradually transformed into something that pleased me very much: a Victorian secret garden with high walls, curved doors, and a peaceful, Old World feel. To my delight, other people began to notice. Tourists stopped by and politely asked if they could see the garden, and soon I opened it to the public. Before long, the garden appeared in *Midwest Living* and *Traverse* magazines. As I weeded and grubbed and as visitors passed through, quirky incidents would sometimes occur; these were too good not to preserve. Then, too, people often asked my advice about gardening, or told me their own lovely stories. I began to write.

At first I wrote just for myself, sometimes shyly showing them to my husband and daughters. But one July day in 2005, after much prodding from Joe, I gathered my courage and walked into the *Traverse City Record-Eagle* newsroom with my first offering. To my delight, the Features editor liked it! I began to blog for the newspaper and write a Sunday column. Nervous, exhilarated and crammed with ideas, I oh-so-gradually found my literary voice, and with her encouragement, dared to venture further afield. Soon I was writing not only about the garden but also about dogs running from trash cans, the inner lives of doors, and shoveling snow in Britain, not to mention the odd ghost. Readers loved them, and the column has now enjoyed five years of publication. Fans have encouraged me to collect them into a book. So I did—and you're holding it in your hands.

I decided to begin by collecting columns about life, in which the garden itself plays a supporting role. Columns about the art of gardening figure only marginally in these selections; they will appear in a future volume.

These articles were originally published in slightly different form (and, in some cases, with different titles) in the *Traverse City Record-Eagle*, as well as in that newspaper's online blog, between 2005 and 2009. Please note that some may seem out of place because I made frequent long trips to England and often wrote about Traverse City while I was abroad—and vice versa. They're presented here more or less in the order in which they appeared in the newspaper.

The *Record-Eagle* has allowed me a long leash, so, of course, I've tugged at it unmercifully, straining these good people to the limit. Their eyebrows nest permanently in their hairlines, and they sigh, but still, they allow me my six impossible grammatical inventions before each weekly publication. I extend heartfelt thanks to Kathy Gibbons, my longtime editor. She believed in me and first invited me to write for the newspaper. Thanks, too, go to Jodee Taylor, my current editor;

and kudos to the unsung people at the copy desk for their patience, guidance and tolerance of my grammatical oddities.

Major thanks go to my husband Joe; my younger daughter Elisabeth, who never stopped believing in me; and to my elder daughter Jenny, who guided me through the book-editing process with consummate skill. And finally, thank you, faithful readers. You encouraged me for years to gather my adventures into book form. I hope you enjoy them as much the second time around.

Fowl Deeds Done in Dead of Night

VILLAINS HAD BEEN DINING ON the Fairy Garden. The evidence was everywhere. Unseemly rips interrupted the lovely, billowy flow of my ground-hugging Irish moss. Torn chunks were flung everywhere. Worse, its delicate surface was full of holes reminiscent of miniature cannonball hits. And the culprits had eaten every last "Etain" violet. Tiny white porcelain fairy-musicians shivered under their bare stems, and a formerly charming scene now looked pathetic. I realized this beak-sized damage constituted fowl play.

Hmmm…Four chunky mallards had been snoozing in the front garden a few days before; later that afternoon I watched them enter the Fairy Garden and look around. That's all they did—look, before waddling away, with soft, quack-mutters suggesting deep thoughts. Shrugging, I'd gone about my business.

Two nights later I'd awakened to muted rustlings and soft grunts, punctuated by occasional squawky burps and other odd noises, but it was 2:00 A.M. and I couldn't be bothered to pad downstairs and check. I knew animals moved around in the garden at night, and though this amount of noise was unusual, they *were* animal sounds.

The next day I learned that ignoring them had cost me.

After stomping around angrily for a bit, I mended the rips, swept away the dislodged dirt, gave up on the larger craters, and calmed down. Surely I could devise a plan to "cook their goose."

The first thing to do was to block off the iron gate, since they were ducking through it to dine at Sunnybank's salad bar. I trotted to the garage and retrieved a board eighteen inches tall, and nearly long enough to cover the gate's length. After adding an old screen and bricks to keep the whole thing from collapsing, I sprayed my inelegant structure with "Deer Away," whose label pictured other invaders, like squirrels and rabbits, successfully repelled. Phew! My fingers dripped with the foul concoction. Wiping them off, I grinned, wolfishly.

That night I slept on the couch. Around midnight, soft, conversational quacks wafted though the opened living room window. I awoke and rushed there. Four fat ducks in a ragged line were waddling confidently to dinner. Exchanged pleasantries ended abruptly in a loud bump, followed immediately by an outraged, shocked squawk! Anticipating, the leader had forgotten to look, and had beaked the board! I hugged myself, delighted, then began a deep, ominous growl, rounded off with a soft howl and loud raspberry, finishing nicely with flashing lights, courtesy of my trusty torch. Alarmed and confused, they ducked and ran, quacking and flapping, to the relative safety of the park across the street. I laughed myself into hiccups, and fell back onto the couch again, not bothering to relocate to my proper bed. This was sweet revenge.

It was a good thing I stayed. More fowl-chat roused me about 5:00 A.M. The wretches were back, noisily discussing the situation, figuring they'd simply mixed up the directions. Approaching warily, one beast beaked the board, then, disgusted, backed away from the ghastly scent. Another indignant soul checked carefully for possible breaches in the barricade. Nope. Quacking disconsolately, they re-treated back across the quiet street into the park in a ragged line, still incredulous, still confused. My fist punched the air; YES!

Just to be certain, I bunked on the couch for two more nights; predictably, the silly quackers returned—to find nothing had changed.

Teeth gleaming in the dark, I plumped my (down) pillow and slept, triumphant.

A Magnificent, Bird-Brained Obsession

FOUR YEARS AGO, A CARDINAL couple decided to raise a family in my insect-rich garden. For weeks, I awoke to their duets as they built their nest, laid eggs, and waited.

One day I noticed Father Bird was wearing out a particular portion of sky, flying back and forth, his beak crammed with squirmy delights for madam. Days later, the children arrived, and the trips tripled.

In the meantime, looking to make the side garden more "reflective," I hung a large mirror on the wall behind the wicker swing, within the huge euonymus bush. It opened the garden wonderfully, doubling its apparent size in a grand trompe l'oeil. I preened.

As I stood back to admire the effect, I noted Father Bird, on his way home, skidding to a stop in mid-air. Something had caught his eye. Feathers fluffing, he backtracked, a beaked bug dangling like an old cigarette. He gulped it down and approached the mirror. Aha! An encroacher, as large as he, and every bit as annoyed. Unacceptable! He'd already claimed this territory. No tick-ridden, moldy-feathered upstart would worm his way in. The cardinal rule was: One Lord Per Manor. Only a feather-brained juvenile would trespass so blatantly.

Our hero flew at him, claws extended, wings full out. Whack! Hmmm...That was one tough rival! Gathering himself, he flew at the intruder again; the clamor reverberated throughout the garden as the bird in the mirror gave as good as he got. Many swoops, pecks, and squawks later, a brief time-out was called. Father sat unsteadily on a bough before the mirror, reflecting. Next time, that interloper would be history...#%@$&*%!

Alas, hours later his topknot was askew, his eyes were blacker than usual, and he took much longer breaks. But he must have noticed that his rival was just as pooped.

Meanwhile, his wife became increasingly annoyed. I heard her call; the kids were hungry—where was he? Secretly relieved, he snatched up lunch and stagger-winged home. But later that afternoon, after downing a quick drink and a few bugs, he cruised to the battleground, certain that that pompous featherhead wouldn't dare stick around after such a thrashing—but there he was! Furious, Father fought valiantly, and, endless pecks and chesty encounters later, he wobbled home, exhausted, only to suffer further henpecking.

Life is so unfair.

Incredibly, that cardinal managed to feed his family, and, even after the kids grew and flew, continued to defend his territory for nearly five months! He defined exhausted determination; Bent-Beak Syndrome was a constant concern.

I tried covering the mirror with a large beach towel, but he wasn't fooled. He'd scream insults, his temper as red-hot as his feathers, and when I'd remove it to open the garden to visitors, the bird in the mirror was always there, just as rumpled and exactly as furious. I dangled a large rubber king snake over the mirror's top, which deterred dad for three days (and unsettled two elderly human visitors), but after a few test swoops, he knew it was a fraud. Ditto for the realistic bob-headed owl I painstakingly wired to a branch.

That bird was obsessed with winning. I decided it must be a guy thing. By October his feathers had a frizzled wilt, his song was off-key, and his wife had left him. Finally, in late fall, he declared the battle a draw and vanished. Wearily wiping away beak and body marks for the hundredth time, I truly understood the meaning of the term "bird brain."

Laughter — Often the Best Medicine

ONE DAY, A TALL ELDERLY man, his slumped posture telegraphing deep sadness, opened the heavy door and walked into the Brick-Walled Garden. He was accompanied by his silent, morose son. Both paused to look around. (I was sitting on the far side, by the last gate; they probably thought I was a visitor.)

It was quiet in that garden. The neighbor's huge basswood tree loomed over the tall garden wall, dropping the occasional yellow leaf. A huge mirror buried in the brick wall reflected tiny flowers and rich moss. There was no breeze, no scurrying of tiny feet, no bird to chirp a greeting.

Suddenly, the older man noticed something: a small circular wall recess with an exquisitely carved bust of a wide-eyed medieval bagpiper. (It's a copy of one found in the crumbling tenth-century stonework of Hereford Cathedral in England; by purchasing it years ago, I'd supported their restoration fund.) He examined every delicate detail. Then, glancing left toward another portion of wall, he stared—and burst out laughing. He really let go! Rust around the edges of that laugh flaked off until only pure mirth was left. His stunned son looked in the direction of his father's pointing finger, and then he understood. More laughter; tension and sadness melted away. Eventually they collected themselves, and, still grinning, moved on. The father wiped his eyes. I heard another low chuckle as they walked past me up the steps and out into the front garden.

As he closed the final gate the younger man turned to me and said, quietly, "It's the first time I've heard him laugh in a year! When Mom died, he took it hard..." His voice trailed off, and he glanced at the retreating figure of his father, who looked back, still smiling, his back erect now. Waving goodbye to me, he joined him.

What they'd found so funny is another small wall decoration near the busy bagpiper. A shaggy-looking fellow has his index finger firmly poked up his nose. Clearly, he disliked the musician's racket. Linking the two busts had amused me, and had certainly hit the spot for this pair. I peered over the gate; they were chatting happily as they ambled toward their car and mimicked that classic gesture.

Though separated by oceans of time and water, these twenty-first-century visitors could still relish a tenth-century cathedral worker's rough rebellion, probably against an obnoxious, corpulent overseer. I imagined that, betting his boss wouldn't climb 150 feet up the dangerous cathedral scaffolding, some grubby, sandaled artist had carved this outrageous self-portrait to express stony disdain.

In any eon, that is powerful medicine.

The Wonderful Rebirth of Three Lives

ONE DAY, CHOPPING VEGETABLES IN the kitchen, I chanced to see an elderly couple wandering through the main garden. She was smiling, commenting on various small things. He had eyes only for her. Suddenly, reaching into his pocket, he brought out a tiny box, hesitated, then nervously turned to face her. She looked confused, standing in the sunlight; he placed it on his palm, then tentatively offered it. I was struck by the emotion he displayed—a combination of love, fear, and hope. She stared at him, completely undone, but then, never taking her eyes off him, she reached for his gift, then slowly opened the velvet box. Inside was a ring. She gasped, looked closer, then carefully removed it and allowed him to place it on her finger. Their hands trembled. For once, nobody was in the garden, just those two. I felt guilty witnessing this private moment, but was unable to tear myself away.

For a long moment neither one spoke; then she hugged him, laughing, and tearful. His face was the picture of relief and joy; hers radiated delight and love. I hugged myself, thrilled to have seen the birth of their new life together.

One spring morning a teacher brought a small class of excited nine-year-olds. They wandered about questioning, exclaiming and pointing. Then, organizing themselves, they burst into song, which brought tears to my eyes. What a perfect gift for the grubby gardener! Later they mailed me wonderful drawings. Through the children's fresh eyes, my garden bloomed anew. I laminated them to use as cherished placemats.

Another time, about four years ago, I was securing rose canes when a young woman rang the garden bell and entered. Something about her demeanor warned me to give her space. She looked pale and fragile, and might have been crying. Sitting on the big bench she wrung her hands, a bundle of nerves. Seeing me some distance away she smiled, and waved good morning, but again, instinct told me not to intrude. Soon she left, looking determined, striding with purpose through the Ram's Head Garden and out the final set of doors. I heard a car start and drive away. Shrugging, I continued my work, but wondered.

One hour later, the same woman re-appeared, but I almost didn't recognize her. The change in her demeanor was remarkable. Her face was luminous. She called me over and told me her story.

"I had all the symptoms of a reappearance of a terrible disease. Tests were done, and the results came back this morning. I saw my doctor just now to hear what they've revealed. I'd hoped to relocate to Arizona with my husband and our child, but this nightmare—this tiger—was going to make me part of him...no new start like we'd been hoping for. But the doctor's told me the tiger is gone, for now. I've been given an extension, thank God, and I'm going to make the most of it!"

She looked calmer now, and breathed deeply, then got up to leave, saying, simply, "Thanks." We exchanged delighted smiles, and she floated out, largely unaware of her surroundings, but somehow sustained by the scents and water music. That encounter made my summer.

Tending flowers reminds me that life is short, death is certain, and love, joy and hope never die. They are the steel threads that secure our fragile, delicate lives, helping us coexist with tigers in the night.

Alien Thoughts in a Foreign Garden

I LIE ON THE WARM earth, eyes closed, utterly relaxed, enjoying the sound of the ocean, and the sound of cypress and palm trees moving with the breeze. Sand and water are all around me. Dolphins leap not far from shore; sandpipers, timing their darts perfectly, mine the minute creatures gifted by the waves. Right now the beach is nearly empty of people.

This whole thing is surreal. Two and a half hours ago Joe and I were in Traverse City, shivering in the thirty-one-degree bare-bones landscape, looking ridiculous in light clothing. After boarding AirTran, which departed bang on time, we rocketed along, assisted by a ninety-knot tailwind. Fort Myers welcomed us with seventy-nine degrees, sixty-five percent humidity, and flat terrain. As I am an arboreal creature, this openness is always an adjustment for me.

A few minutes later my sister drove us to their condo in Naples, and we walked to the nearby beach to stretch our legs. They live close to a state park, where I am now.

The vegetation here is shockingly different. This early in the season, floral scents aren't prominent, but there *is* color. Pinks and violets and shocking reds surround me amid fascinating foliage. Lizard-like, I absorb the heat of the day, and listen.

Seagulls scream overhead. The ground shakes from the thumping of giant pilings being driven deep into the earth farther down the beach signal the relentless construction of ever-taller condos, sold before they are formed, their ghostly promise already worth more than what the buyers paid.

Just behind me, across the park road, lies a tangled bewilderment of low Florida swamp cypress. It reminds me of a Dr. Seuss land-scape gone crazy. Though it looks impenetrable, many animals call it home—including panthers. There were signs along the road that read: Warning: Panther Crossing. Gulp. I imagine contemplative predators watching me. The hair rises on my neck. For a long moment I refuse to open my eyes. Reluctantly, heart beating too fast, I look—and meet the unblinking stare of a six-inch long lizard perched on my chest atop my paperback book, perhaps eight inches from my face. How has it managed this without my knowing? Its calm gaze is shocking. The lizard is studying me, thinking. I stare back, and we size each other up.

He thinks, "Hmmm. Too big to eat, too still to be threatening, too stupid to run, too recently down to attract flies; therefore, not interesting."

I think: "Is it poisonous? Will it bite? Why isn't it afraid? Are there more on me that I can't see? Why me?"

He thinks, "Why not?"

We both think: "Not edible. But alien…"

After a while I begin to relax, and admire that dinosaur-like body, those googly eyes, which seem to move independently, and that scaly, slash-mouthed half-smile, as he ponders me. His body rises and falls, like the ocean, as I breathe...Suddenly the bushes are disturbed, and my husband comes upon me. The lizard disappears. In an instant he is simply gone, taking his thoughts, but leaving me with a hundred questions.

My own garden is crammed full of mysteries, but it's a part of the comfortable world I know, and think I dominate. Florida reminds me, a brief guest on planet Earth, that I am woefully ignorant of life outside my small space.

Florida keeps me humble.

Masked Bandits and Peeping Toms

ONE COLD WINTER NIGHT ABOUT 2:00 A.M., I awoke suddenly, hearing muttering and scratching noises. Still sleep-fogged, I lay there listening. Had I been dreaming? My husband slept on, oblivious.

Sure enough, there were those sounds again—and heavy breathing. Someone was expending a lot of effort trying to pry apart the bedroom screen! (We'd left the storm window off, because we enjoyed fresh cold air.)

Tense and alert now, I quietly rose and felt around for a weapon, while marveling that a burglar would attempt to gain entry from the icy porch roof. How? Did he bring a ladder? No, patrol cars would spot it. My mind raced. Grappling hooks, then? No significant snow had fallen lately, but it was still dangerous, especially in the dark. (There was no moon tonight.)

I woke my husband and quickly explained the situation, suggesting we call the police before dealing with the situation our own way. He nodded, signaled "wait," and took charge. (Joe's an ex-Marine.) After listening a minute, he whispered that our small noises hadn't deterred the invader, who'd carried on working, unconcerned. Something about that persistence didn't make sense. Grabbing a heavy flashlight he crept to the window, and, taking a deep breath, turned it on. There, peering in, hands resting on the screen while cupping his eyes, was our culprit—a huge raccoon, mask in place, unfazed by the light. He calmly looked us up and down, and I thought I saw disappointment in those canny, intelligent eyes.

We moved closer to get a better look. This beast was huge—Joe reckoned twenty or twenty-five pounds. He probably lived across the street in Hannah Park, alongside the Boardman River—a good choice, based on that girth.

Coons are powerful, persistent, smart, and incredibly curious. He would eventually have managed to get inside. It was a graphic reminder to always secure that window when we weren't actually occupying the room. We'd read of the damage raccoons could do; it made us shudder.

After a while he sighed, pulled away, and made a comment to someone behind. Heavens, there were two! The second fat 'coon assumed the position, studying us as though we were specimens. Both looked longingly at the room, imagining, I suppose, what fun it could have been.

Another resigned sigh—no strange new world to explore tonight— then they turned to go. We were intrigued to see how they'd managed the ascent; my husband shined the flashlight on their departing bottoms, and gasped. There weren't two raccoons, there were three, four, five, six—seven! of the huge beasts, sitting up there in an orderly row, hands on knees, backs against the wall. Two of them wrestled playfully while waiting their turn to view the aliens. Each studied us intently, hands-to-screen, fascinated; then indulged in a long, slow survey of the room. Then they reluctantly followed the others down the thirty-foot tall Japanese lilac tree, which trembled and swayed as each well-fed 'coon descended its trunk backwards. It was a toss-up whether the straining branches would hold those great bodies. But their descent was unhurried, orderly, and without incident.

We rushed downstairs to see them ambling toward the park in a loose, chatty group. Somewhere down the block a dog barked in a frenzied way, probably catching their scent. The raccoons ignored it. The last one turned to look wistfully at our alien structure before blending into the darkness.

Nature's children were thwarted in their quest for a close encounter of the third kind.

This time.

Train of Thought

LIFE CAN HANG BY SUCH a tenuous thread. A human being, perfectly healthy one minute, is gone, utterly, the next. This thought repeated itself as I sat sadly in the halted, silent Chicago-bound Amtrak train on a crisp and sunny mid-autumn morning.

Joe and I had boarded the huge train about three-quarters of the way down its enormous length and departed Flint around 7:00 A.M. I gazed through reasonably clean windows at the mostly unlovely landscape. Scruffy trees, nearly stripped of leaves, lined roads and fence lines; some were laced with smidgens of snow. The pungent smell of coffee and microwaved food wafted through the air from the dining car behind ours. A large, cheerful group of middle-aged ladies exchanged cookies, hot chocolate and gossip; they had plans for the Windy City, by golly. My husband listened to iPod music next to me; two charming primary-school children stopped by our seats and announced that their parents were taking them to see King Tut. The eight-year-old boy pointed to Mom and Dad, who waved at us, amused.

The sun shone stronger as the morning wore on; our speed, around thirty MPH, wouldn't set any records.

The train was not quite two hours out of Flint when suddenly, inexplicitly, deep in the countryside, it groaned; brakes were applied, and slowly, oh, so slowly, the monster stopped. Over the loudspeaker came a calm, very brief announcement. There was an emergency. We would be indefinitely delayed.

Bewildered, we scanned the aisles, then peered out the windows; everything looked just fine. Suddenly, the air was filled with sirens. We watched, amazed, as fire trucks, an ambulance, and lots of police cars lined one side of the train, just outside. Firemen crawled under the car behind ours, and there was much arm-waving and walkie-talkie conversation. Clearly, something terrible had happened.

My husband quietly offered his services as a physician, but the conductor shook her head, sadly. "I'm afraid the poor man is dead." Apparently he'd been walking down the middle of the tracks, deeply engrossed in whatever he was listening to; earphones covered his ears. The engineer had seen the fellow from a long way back and sounded the whistle, over and over. The train's intense rail-vibrations, the conductor said, would have been hard to miss. The engineer had grown increasingly desperate. He knew the physics: it would be impossible to stop in time. The earphoned man had continued walking, head down in concentration, his back to the train; the next instant he'd vanished under its massive nose. His body was found under the dining car, all that incredibly long way down its length.

After perhaps three hours, we were allowed to go our way. The man's remains had been retrieved, with great difficulty; police and a National Transportation Safety Board inspector had questioned relevant people; the area was cleaned up, and most officialdom had finally departed.

The conductor remarked that train accidents, especially those involving cars, had occurred with distressing frequency during her long tenure. People lost in thought; chatting on cell phones; or distracted by pets, children, or alcohol, would forget to pay attention. Their cars were as butter under unstoppable megatons of iron and steel.

Infrequently, individuals would get caught, as this man was, striding between the rails on a clear, sunny day, perhaps lost in the deep, throbbing bass of hard rock, or maybe profoundly interested in a story, or lecture…

He'd ended in a blink.

Freezertown

CHICAGO. IT'S SO COLD HERE that buses won't start, so the schools are closed. It's so cold that breath freezes on face scarves, and thighs quickly become chunks of ice. It's so incredibly cold that the streets are full of abandoned cars, which had simply given up. Officials have warned everyone to stay home, if possible.

I'm here to cook and clean for my exhausted oldest daughter, in her senior year of residency at University of Chicago hospital. She has no time to eat, shop, wash, iron, or do normal tasks; she comes home after fifteen hours of non-stop doctoring and collapses into bed after downing a few bites of something nourishing. This insane existence ends June 31, when, at a stroke, she'll have a normal life.

I could tell you terrifying stories, but will content myself with just one thing. If you find yourself in a teaching hospital, ask this one question of the physicians treating you. "How long has it been, Doctor, since you slept at least six hours?" Just ask. Do it firmly. Most especially, ask the residents. You'll be shocked.

When chores are done, I walk for miles. The cold doesn't bother me. I wear long underwear under my cargo pants, three layers under my thick sweater, then two down coats, two scarves, a down hood, and thick socks and mittens. I am a short, snug, round green polar bear and I find the whole thing exhilarating.

I moved to Traverse City because I love the seasons, and Chicago is part of the Midwestern extreme-weather experience. Fearsome, icy winds drop the temperature to minus ten Fahrenheit, but I stride out, hop buses, walk the length of Michigan Ave. (perhaps five miles), check out the wonderful nineteenth-century architecture, and admire the magnificent library façade. Once in a while I pop into Caribou Coffee to sip a hot brew or request a mug of hot water. Cheerful attendants seem amused by my "order."

One day I literally bumped into a street person. She had bulging bags of treasures dangling from her arms; more stout bags were attached to a large backpack. She looked me up and down, and then laughed a rich, mostly toothless belly laugh. "You as round as you is tall, girl. How you see?" I grinned, liking her immediately. Together we strolled into a Caribou coffee shop, where I bought us two lattes.

Her name was Irma, and she loved downtown Chicago in all its moods. She'd lived in the city, on the edge, for twenty-two years. She sipped her drink thoughtfully, comfortable with silence. Finally, she turned and said; "Library's warm. Early is best. Don't nobody notice my sort." Another pause. "Why you out?"

Why, indeed. I took my time, blowing on the coffee, and then grinned.

"Why not?"

She laughed again, showing a few dark teeth. The reply pleased her. We sat there, watching people hurry past the window, and shared a cookie. She told me she'd been to a concert "over at the bus stop. Frien' plays a hot clarinet. Ah gets mellowed out."

Music—oh, boy! My passion. We exchanged blues favorites, and mourned Billie Holiday and Satchmo. She kept banging my padded arm to emphasize points. I admired her beautiful headscarf, which had bass fiddles all over it, portrayed in burnished brown colors that complimented her dark skin. "This here's a gift—it jus' blew by," she grinned. "Them's the best sort."

Soon it was time to move on. We ambled out, two overstuffed, waddling, layered bundles, and parted with big smiles and waves. She disappeared without looking back.

An Airborne Visitation

A delicious day is one that is not entirely predictable.—Anonymous

WELL. JUST WHEN I'D ASSUMED this day would end as countless others have—I'd finish my brisk Chicago evening walk, go home, sleep—the Imp of the Perverse roused itself, yawned, grinned, and flicked a long finger.

Here's a true tale, full of sound and slurry, signifying nothing.

I'd fed my exhausted, cold-sick oldest daughter a plump chicken dinner, and after a critical inspection, decided she needed a walk through Chicago's charming neighborhood downtown area, a block from our door. Trapped in the bowels of the University of Chicago Hospital Emergency Department for weeks, she needed to breathe in clean lake air. Dr. Jenny had the next twenty-four hours to herself; even her pager was peaceful. She and I relaxed into the rhythm of a lovely evening stroll. Destination? Borders Books, a long trot down Broadway. Incurable bookworms that we were, we twitched with anticipation.

Something was missing, though. I couldn't put my finger on exactly what.

A lovely half-moon glowed in a black sky. We passed interesting store windows, imaginatively decorated. The usual, mercifully muted thump-thump instrumental noise leaked from their merchandise-stuffed interiors onto the sidewalk. Even now, at nearly 8:00 P.M., lots of cheerful thirtysomethings were delighting in the relative warmth. It was a welcome change from the incredible cold of the last few weeks.

Suddenly, there was a whoosh of air, then a definitive, sucking *plop!* With a confident, perfectly balanced landing, a pink rubber toilet plunger touched down in the exact center of the street. It teetered, took a firm grip, and did what it was designed to do—create a vacuum.

Even for Chicago, this was stunning. People paused in mid-stride, gaping. Everything went quiet.

Here began the toilet plunger's fifteen minutes of fame. It basked in the glow of the street lamp. For a long moment, nobody moved. Then, almost as a beautifully choreographed unit, people looked up. No planes flew overhead. The big buildings along the wide street displayed darkened, firmly shut higher-storied windows, well away from the street.

There was absolutely no rational explanation for this dubious miracle.

Eyeing the pink, alien exclamation point, many onlookers realized they could have been targeted. Nervously people took a step back, eyes in constant motion, trying to make sense of this. The toilet plunger hung on, stiffly erect, thrilled by this unprecedented attention.

Abruptly, a sharp, passing breeze made its tall wooden handle sway; the rubber mouth sighed, disconnected, and the hapless plunger toppled to the pavement, rudely exposing an unlovely, suspiciously darker underside. The spell was broken.

Everyone laughed till tears came, and as Jenny and I held our sides and roared with the rest of them, I realized that this was what had been missing.

Sometimes life should be outrageous; this absurd "visitation" fit the bill; not one passerby really wanted to understand. It was enough that it had happened, right here in Chicago. Mopping our eyes, we moved on, appreciating that, for one gripping moment, we'd been plunged into the Twilight Zone.

Winter Meditations

Better a little with content than much with contention. —Anonymous

TODAY, IN CHICAGO, I ENTERTAINED well-deep thoughts after a bracing three-mile walk to buy groceries. My backpack and I battled sleet, freezing rain, blowing snow and howling, pane-rattling winds. Down-bundled and snug, I relished every minute. For me, seasonal outrages keep Complacency, the child of Familiarity, at bay.

For Irma, the street lady I met the other day, Chicago in three seasons means breathing clean lake air, admiring bright flower stands on corners, and relishing the lovely crunch of beach sand under her bare, or sandaled, feet. She's learned to adapt to winter's special challenges, and actually thrive. While refusing to discuss particulars, she admitted the intense cold keeps her sharp.

Good boots are essential. She enjoys hunting down the right footgear in thrift shops, as properly shod feet are key to comfortably managing her life.

Odd jobs—passing out circulars, breaking down big store packing boxes, sweeping—pay just enough to move in and around Chicago by bus. Her friends are scattered around its huge girth.

She saves warm museums and other public buildings for fascinating winter explorations. Irma lives in the moment, but gently welcomes every fresh day, "'cause they's always different."

She told me she found peace of mind, "sudden-like" in a huge trash container, many winters ago. As she sorted through it for boxed, discarded pizza slices, she realized that as long as people ate too much, then threw away perfectly good food, she'd never starve. "Ya jus' has to know when an' where to look…" Eating for Irma is an adventure, especially now.

This lady described herself as happy. She expects nothing, delights in little things, and has nothing much to guard. "Ah sleeps good. Worry don't follow me."—a fractional pause—"Taxes don't, neither." And she winked.

Sometimes a contented life can be that simple.

Requiem for a Fruit Fly

"AHHHH...IT'S SO CLEAR OUTSIDE today." I breathed deeply near the screened window of my daughter's fifth-floor Chicago apartment—and a fruit fly flew up my nose! I reeled back, instantly realizing I'd been the target of another fly-kamikaze mission. These wretched specks had attached me twice before, zeroing in on my eyes.

This time, though, cheering spectator-flies must have been delighted by my nose-snatching, off-balance stumble into a pile of packages and suitcases. Poof! A bag of Kenya AA fine-ground coffee split open; its contents sprayed everywhere. When I'd disentangled myself from straps, coffee grounds, and music books, I was angry! I shook my fists, hollered, and said words no decent woman should say...

Alas. Fruit fly fury is—well, fruitless.

They must devise these spectacular suicides as a way of making their brief lives count. I mean, what worthwhile goals can fruit flies strive for? They're not around long enough to do more than think a thought, are they?

Many's the time I've smacked my own face in a futile attempt to annihilate them. A mischievous dot would meander across my book page, distracting me from the text, and enjoy my confusion as I'd try to distinguish it from the floaters in my eye.

Hmmm, I thought, fuming. Clearly, I'm smarter than a fruit fly. These were certainly doomed, because I understand, and can operate, tools. First, though, I had to clean up the coffee mess. After that I'd eliminate any fly stupid enough to show itself. The vacuum shrieked as I held the hose like a machine gun. A female Rambo was on the prowl.

After a thorough purge, I collapsed onto the couch, reasonably sure I had at least unnerved them. The apartment smelled vaguely of coffee, hot machinery, and agitated dust. I needed a drink. A glass of cold water smoothed me nicely. But then, out of the blue, another determined fruit fly took aim at my apparently irresistible snout. This time, though, I was prepared. As it nose-dived, I struck, quick as a snake. A minute black corpse, centered on my palm, confirmed the kill. Vaguely ashamed of my own elation, I muttered *"Requiescat in pace"* and washed it down the drain.

Small triumphs like this can make my day.

Chaos at Caribou Coffee

I LURCHED INTO A CARIBOU Coffee shop in Chicago, glad to set down my heavy grocery bags, which were causing hand-cramp and a distinct tilt in my walk. An injection of leaded brew, and maybe even a hunk of their delicious lemon poppyseed cake, would set me straight. I sipped, munched, and happily fell into Miss Marple's world, as she solved the mystery of The Body in the Library without dropping a stitch.

Gradually, the conversation of two stocky, casually dressed fiftysomething men sitting next to me captured my attention. Certain trigger words were impossible to ignore. They spoke as though I were invisible, but we were practically knocking elbows.

"...She's sixteen, Frank, a virgin till she got herself entangled with the guy, who's old-money, and after she was sick a lot a school friend told her to get tested—she's positive for HIV. And her parents have no idea."

"My God—her father'll kill him! How'd you find out? Did Jake tell you?"

"Yeah... too bad; both families will be devastated. What a chaotic situation... Money can't fix this nightmare."

"No, but nowadays there's treatment. It isn't always a death sentence, is it? Look at Magic Johnson."

Sounds of coffee slurping… a cough, then…

"What happened with that multiple murder?"

"Another mess. The cops are finding cocaine connections… I got the kids placed temporarily. The eight-year old boy's a handful. And, I think the oldest kid knows something. She doesn't say much— gets nightmares a lot. There's suspicion of past abuse. I'm checking hospitals to see if she's had 'accidents' before. The parents say they don't know why the killings happened, but they don't meet my eyes. The whole thing stinks…."

There was no attempt to muffle their voices. I decided they'd lost their instinct for discretion from sheer weariness, after years of wrestling with ruined people.

Suddenly, I wished myself anywhere else. I dumped the napkin, returned the coffee mug, gathered my bags and escaped, marveling that two professionals would speak so freely, in a public place, about private horror and murder.

Half way down the block I realized I'd forgotten my mittens.

Sighing, I retraced my steps, and retrieved them. The men were still talking. The guy sitting at the other little table looked uncomfortable.

Too much reality, I thought as I hurried away, more than coffee-jittered.

Dive! Dive! Robin Attacks a Hood!

TODAY I WATCHED THE ROBUST robin's neck feathers bristle: he'd sensed something wicked stalking his mate, and him. Nervous, both stopped building their nest and flew to the alley telephone wires to scan the area. Yes! There! A huge gray-backed cat was poised right on the edge of the garage rooftop; slitted yellow eyes were locked onto their half-built home a few yards from the rooftop. The Beast was motionless, except for the tip of his tail, which twitched ominously, giving silent voice to his intentions. Those claws, long, sharp, and deadly, dug into the roof tiles; the well-fed body was still. The robins knew that cat. They'd seen other hapless residents efficiently dispatched last year. They knew what would happen if they ever lost concentration and allowed that stealthy monster to sneak up on them.

Exactly then, an agitated squirrel squawked an alarm from the fence top; the whole garden knew something was about to go down. Chippie vanished; mourning doves ceased cooing—the air was electric. The male robin shifted his body and fluffed his wings, knowing he had but one choice: ATTACK!—or lose it all. Without pausing to think he launched himself, flying directly at the stalker, beak pointing the way, throwing every ounce of strength and speed into this first, crucial dive.

Cat, caught in an exposed position, realized the angry bird wouldn't hesitate to rake him. Fat garden worms had provided strength; now outrage fueled the bird's dive.

Before he could process what was happening, Robin was upon him, claws extended, wings balanced. Cat felt needles barely rake his furred spine. Hunched, he backed away from the edge and up the roof ridge slightly. Fangs gleamed as he snarled, more annoyed than afraid. Seeing the small retreat, Robin took heart and made another pass, then another, giving voice to his rage. Each swoop forced the feline back another inch. The intense barrage was probably embarrassing.

Cat found it difficult to anticipate the different attack angles. Some came from right out of the mid-morning sun, some from the south; all threatened his unprotected back. Off balance, reluctant to swat at Robin up there on the roof, Cat gathered his tattered dignity and moved to the overhanging maple tree, then backed down carefully, doing his best to ignore the furious robin, who continued his assault— master, for now, of the situation.

I looked up, admiring the stunning aerobatics, then looked back: Cat had vanished.

Robin finally perched, exhausted, on the high wire, with his mate close by. Together they huddled up there, silent, knowing it wasn't over, but committed now. She had eggs to deliver; their big nest was nearing completion. Life, for many weeks, was going to be incredibly difficult. Predators were everywhere. Winds and lashing rains could make nesting a misery; spring frosts were possible. Constant vigilance was paramount; sleep would be a luxury. Providing the massive amounts of food necessary to sustain the coming family would severely test their resolve.

But the rewards were immense.

If they made no serious mistakes their children would grow strong, then leave home consummate avians. They'd find mates of their own, bring forth children, and protect them just as fiercely. The lineage would continue.

Heartened by the temporary victory, the female continued to add mossy finishing touches to their home, while father robin kept a wary vigil.

For the moment, at least, with the young day's sun on their wings, life was good.

A Titanic Challenge for Nobody Special

Never, never, never, never give up. —Winston Churchill

YESTERDAY, AS I WAS GATHERING up lawnmower-disabling twigs and pinecones that littered the lawn from recent winds, my eye was caught by something decidedly odd. Near the edge of the sidewalk lay a huge, dead insect. Its color, an electric blue-green, was still vivid for this part-bee, part-dragonfly, part-grasshopper. Frankly, I couldn't decide what it was. Six legs poked stiffly out. But here's the thing: it seemed to be moving, ever so slightly. Intrigued, I watched. There was no wind, no reason for the motion I'd detected. I nudged it…yep. Dead as a mackerel.

I settled back to ponder this mini-mystery.

There—it moved again! On hands and knees, with my nose to the ground (good thing dead bugs don't stink), I was astonished to see an ant—a very small ant—dragging the giant bug. That ant was the size of a fat period, but he was huffing and puffing, putting his all into shifting that enormous carcass. Micro-millimeter by micro-millimeter he was making progress. By tomorrow he'd manage perhaps another few inches. I carefully searched for a nest in the grass: there was nothing for three feet in any direction. But his agonizingly slow, focused persistence indicated that Ant knew exactly where he was going with his titanic prize. Eventually he'd drag it down his home-hole. Everyone would high-antenna him, then feast on megabug protein; aphids would provide dessert. (These highly complex creatures routinely enslave aphids, and milk them for the honeydew they secrete. The aphids benefit, as ants offer protection from predators.)

I could almost see his mind working.

"Let's see—if I run back here and push the back end, then dash up to the antennas and pull, then hurry over to the abdomen...'

Busily calculating, then lifting and shifting, had to be wearing him down. But he had a goal; he'd meet it, somehow. Never mind that this prize was immense, while he was minute; never mind that a giant foot could, at any moment, instantly obliterate him; never mind that his home was far, far away, deep in the jungle of gigantic green grass blades looming just ahead. (If it was difficult now to shift Bugzilla, imagine what he'd face two inches from now; those dead, stiffened legs would surely snag on the grass—heavens!) He had no family or friends to help, no way to phone home. Ant was on his own.

Puff. Groan. Shove—Movement! See? Persevere; never give up.

Perhaps he'd pondered his options.

"Well, I could abandon the body, and run home to summon help... But then other clans might claim it, and there goes dinner. Not an option.

"I could wait for rain; water drops would mean less friction, and, if there were a really good downpour, this whole endeavor would be dead easy. All I'd have to do is guide the corpse—but rain isn't predicted any time soon. Not an option.

"I could assume that some of the clan will eventually follow my scent trail and lend a jaw..."

(Ants exemplify teamwork. This option, I decided, had been accepted as the most likely.)

A peculiar sensation crept over me. This creature was moving an object a hundred times his own weight. To not move it, or become discouraged, didn't occur to him. I was deeply impressed by Ant's ability to plan, his inexhaustible enthusiasm, and his refusal to cry "Uncle." Clearly he relished the challenge.

This tiny speck of life made me feel small.

Checking again, just an hour later, I shivered in awe; ant and mega-corpse had vanished!

"Memories...light the corners of my mind..."

IT WAS A LOVELY SUMMER afternoon. An outsized van drove up and unloaded seven Alzheimer's patients, three in wheelchairs, for a scheduled garden tour. The group was mostly silent as they gathered the gate. One or two patients asked where they were, needing confirmation that they were "on track," and that their driver wouldn't forget how to get home. One elderly man hoped aloud, over and over, that he'd turned the stove off before leaving. Their caretakers kept up reassuring, cheerful conversation; before long, they'd settled everyone in the main garden. One wheelchair patient was bent nearly double; the two others stared straight ahead, their hands restlessly picking at the blankets on their laps, not seeming to notice, or care, where they were. Some made their tentative way to the benches and arranged themselves with care. A small lady took hold of the bench arm and, needing its solidity, seemed reluctant to let it go. She looked confused and tensely alert. "Did I turn off the stove?" came a soft voice again.

Mama Nature was feeling benevolent today. Her soft breath ruffled the big grasses and delicate flowers just enough to release their scents. Birds sang, and the air hummed with the buzz of busy insects. The whole garden was a jumble of colors: bright reds, intense pinks, rich golds, and pale or deep blues blended with oranges and purples. Pure white alyssum wound through the beds; its perfume was everywhere. The fountains burbled, their soft murmur muting the rough blat of the outside world. The caregivers chatted quietly among themselves and with the patients.

Gradually I watched these visitors began to respond to Nature in her best mood. Fragments of an old song rose from a woman with a blanket over her knees. The bench sitters made comments addressed to no one about the sights and sounds around them. Three others shyly began to explore.

But something special was happening to one slim, wheelchair-bound man. He sat up straight, looked around with bright eyes, smiled, and began to talk. "Ummm...those rosemary leaves are delicious! I know all about that plant!" Then, pointing to a particularly beguiling daylily: "This wonderful peach color reminds me of Jean's summer dress. I often pick the best blue irises for my mother; she buries her face in them, and thanks me, laughing, because I get them from the neighbor's ditch." More quietly: "I love the summer sniffs because it means no school for two long months....We'll ride the donkey....I have a garden, but it's partly my sister's, too. I can grow just about any veggie, but flowers capture me." Grinning: "We take snapdragons on picnics, and make them 'talk...'"

The staff surrounded him, sharing their own experiences; Mr. Jones replied lucidly, and pointed out his favorite plants. By now the others, their apprehensions forgotten, were exploring and commenting. The woman who had clung to the bench felt secure enough to stand up and move away, nodding and smiling, lost in a world of her own. Even the soft-voiced, stove-worried man sniffed appreciatively as he recalled aloud the lovely kitchen bouquets his wife once gathered from their own garden.

Too soon, it was time to go.

A staff member came over to thank me, taking my hand. "This is truly a special day," he said. "Mr. Jones, in that wheelchair, has never spoken. It's a marvelous resurrection; we couldn't believe our ears. He's so articulate—so full of vivid memories!" He shook his head. "Amazing! The staff won't believe this!"

As the van pulled away, Mr. Jones was still talking. I wandered back into the perfumed garden, deeply content, recalling Shakespeare's Hamlet, to Ophelia: "There's rosemary, that's for remembrance..."

Yarns and Small Tails

ONE FINE, SUNNY JULY AFTERNOON, two elderly women rang the big North Gate bell and entered the main secret garden. They wore sandals, floppy hats, and baggy pants, and their arms were filled with bundles. After much discussion and arm-waving they unfolded two small chairs in dappled shade beside a heavy cooler. They were there to sit and knit, armed with two large clear plastic bags bulging with fat, gaily-colored yarn-balls and long blue knitting needles poking out the top. Comfortably settled in front of an array of flowers, they began to knit rapidly, all the while staring at the blossoms. Lady Two concentrated on a particularly large oriental lily; when the breeze carried its scent past her twitching nose she would pause, close her eyes, and breathe long and deeply. Nobody spoke.

Fountains sang, needles clicked, peace reigned.

Suddenly, Lady One leaped up with a stifled cry; something had just brushed past her feet. Then, enchanted, she pointed her knitting needles toward the thick foliage in front of her. Motioning for her companion to remain seated, she mouthed "bunny," making a hopping V sign that symbolized Elmer Fudd's "wetched wabbit."

"Rats!" I muttered. "There goes the 'elephant ears.' Where's that darn cat when I need him?" Their response was to clickity-knit grey into their designs, grinning all the while.

I knew that rabbit. He'd nibbled one helpless huge-leafed *Colocasia* almost to the ground, clearly finding the stems delicious. I wanted to rush over there and dose the plant with the horribly stinky Deer-Off spray I'd purchased for a million dollars. That stuff seems to work— but as my guests were deep into their yarn-painting, I hesitated. Knitting was serious business. Fouling the air would upset their noses and needles, which looked sharp, I mused with a grin. Sighing, I resigned myself to the possible sacrifice of an ear for art.

The garden bell rang loudly, signaling visitors; it ruffled them not at all. People paused to examine the ladies' work and offered comments or praise. Everyone chatted amicably, but those needles never stopped clicking...

Suddenly Lady Two yelped and gave a violent start, nearly falling off her chair. Needles and yarn tumbled onto the grass as she stood and looked down, frantically shaking her pants. That gesture told me all I needed to know. Chippie, checking for cat sign, had momentarily lost his concentration and collided with her leg, completely unraveling the woman. (I remembered all too well when he'd zipped up my pant leg five years ago, with the cat in hot pursuit.) Now, with an embarrassed chitter and a snap of his tail, the wee beastie vanished, as chipmunks do so well.

The woman said, shakily, "What was THAT?" The other ventured, tentatively, "A rat?"

Recognizing an entrance cue when I hear one, I sailed to the scene, saying, "It's only the chipmunk..."

Both knitted their brows, then burst out laughing. They looked around while sorting out the rainbow-colored yarn-jumble, wondering what else might materialize under their feet. I grinned; the General (what I've dubbed the tulip tree) might not be able to resist lobbing a heavy seed casing or two from vast heights. A bonk to their heads would add the final touch to a garden drama only nature could dream up.

I said as much to the unsettled women, who looked up nervously, then chuckled, good sports to the end. They put away their knitting-things and settled in to eat, re-living and embellishing their adventure amid knee-slapping hoots of laughter.

This small tale would keep their friends in stitches.

On the Very Edge of Flight

SUCH A LOVELY MORNING! I glanced out the kitchen window, and noticed a girl of perhaps thirteen standing in the main garden near the big bench, her right arm held above her head, talking—to herself? No, wait…She was apparently speaking to something on her finger! Hmmm.

I watched from the kitchen as the new sun bathed the child in honeyed light, and then I padded quietly outside to investigate. There, an amazing sight greeted me. A magnificent Monarch butterfly delicately hung, upside down, on her index finger. Its wings gently opened and closed, and the morning sun caught their jeweled colors; the effect was stunning. Accepting my presence with equanimity, she addressed it softly. "It won't be long now; you'll love this garden."

I sat on the bench, momentarily silenced by this astonishing picture. Her sweet smile warmed me.

"She's just emerged from her cocoon, and needs the sun to dry her wings; soon she'll fly away." Her voice was clear, soft, so as not to alarm the butterfly, and devoid of "you know," "I mean," "like," and other horrid verbal tics that infest so much American conversation.

Rarely do I encounter children with such self-possession, and the quiet confidence that normally comes with age and experience. This child fit comfortably into her skin, and was utterly unself-conscious. That gorgeous butterfly dangled contently on her finger, so trusting, and as patient as she, waiting for The Moment.

Her name was Esprit, and she, like her name, was lovely. Her perfect creamy skin glowed with summer sun and youth, and her warm, dark blonde, silky hair fell neatly below her shoulders. Her eyes had a direct gaze that married nicely with that calm, confident voice. "She needs time to adjust to her new world, usually about two or three hours. I live quite near here, and thought your garden, with its relative safety, would be a fine place to release her. There's certainly a nectar feast here, with lots of different flavors to sample." She moved carefully to a lily, and gently coaxed the creature onto the flower. It clung there for a moment, but seemed hesitant, preferring Esprit's finger. Patiently she allowed the insect to return to its perch, and continued to speak to it quietly, full of encouragement.

After a time she commented: "When her wings harden, flight, and her new life, will be possible. She's chosen the perfect day to emerge; it's warm, with no wind to muss the wonderful, perfumed air." Another direct look, and a radiant smile. This child knew her place in the universe.

We sat together on that bench, content to silently admire the Monarch.

Eventually the garden bell rang; four visitors entered, then stopped in astonishment. I filled them in. Everyone was enchanted, as she explained that for the last couple of years she'd been collecting cocoons spotted on her frequent nature walks. Each time a butterfly would emerge, in her room at home, she'd bring it into Sunnybank Garden.

The visitors were full of questions that Esprit carefully answered. Then, after another quick assessment, she gently settled the insect onto a fresh rose blossom; it seemed happy enough, this time, to remain.

With a final murmured goodbye she stepped away, having done all she could.

Esprit herself had just left the safe, small world of elementary school; her metamorphosis into a high schooler was imminent. She hoped to study veterinary medicine one day. Like the butterfly, the young woman inside her was waiting, calmly, and with great anticipation, for her time to fly.

The Garden, a Lady, a Life Remembered

A LIGHT RAIN DRIZZLED DOWN, running off the limp-leafed Harry Lauder Hazel, and freshening the big hibiscus tree's lovely white blooms. Maybe today I'd catch a break and not have to hand-water my flowers so often. I padded outside, relishing the garden's clean, shining aspect. My mother would say everyone had had their faces washed.

There's a space where the pussy willow tree, a personal favorite, used to be; I'd finally cut it down, as weeks of heat had fried its leaves past the point of recovery. Now the view had opened up, and I suddenly decided that I wouldn't obstruct it again. The daylilies looked delighted to bask in so much light, and the path to the Library Garden was more inviting. I had a renewed appreciation that "less is more."

Ding....The gate bell rang, rather timidly. After a pause, the door creaked open. A tiny, ancient woman entered, just as the sun made a weak attempt to shine. She was gaunt and pale, and wore a pencil-straight dress decorated with embroidery. She began to pick her way across the lawn, pausing often to look around and nod. Entering the Ram's Head Garden, she stopped, lifted her elegant brass-and-ivory cane, and pointed it at me. "You know," she said, after we'd exchanged greetings, "this garden reflects my life. The gnarled tree at its beginning symbolizes my father's arthritis, which was severe." She chuckled. "It never defeated him. He always had a joke up his sleeve—he loved life, and was always laughing."

"Those little impatiens along the path remind me of myself when I was very young." She smiled. "I drove my mother mad."

"Then, further along, you've planted those delightful cannas. They remind me of my teen years. My friends and I were carefree and full of fun. Lord, we were so smooth-skinned!" Her eyes twinkled in her wrinkled face. "And I was certainly taller than I am now, by four inches, and sleek as a seal. I lived in Georgia—I still do—and I favored bright red hats, like the cannas' silly flowers.

"That graceful grass over there—the way it moves....It brings to mind all the dances we used to go to. That's where I met my husband, by the way. We were married 65 years. He died last fall." She paused, gathered herself, and went on, smiling. "That multi-blooming rose bush represents our five wonderful children, and their children, who light up my life. They've certainly known thorny times, but they always manage to cope, and even blossom."

She coughed, smiled at me, and made her way to the bench, and sat with a sigh.

Hoping she would continue, I said, "I've never thought of the garden in quite this way before. Do go on."

Nodding, she continued, in a softer voice. "Those vines that cascade over the back fence bring to mind the overwhelming times, when life seemed too confusing or too complicated. It was one disaster after another, and the only thing we had to keep us sane was Henry's optimism. He always said, 'This, too, shall pass; we will endure.' He was right. We paddled on, and sure enough, the water always calmed."

"If I take this metaphor further, I'm close, now, to the final gate. But that's all right. I don't mind. Life's a trip, as Henry would say, and I'm tired. It's still interesting, and full of challenges that won't end just because I'm about to." She laughed. "Getting up each morning is its own adventure." She coughed again, smiled, and rose to leave.

"That hydrangea just outside the final gate is the promise of things to come....Thanks, my dear, for the scrapbook."

Crotchety Crank, Hammocky Howls

MAYBE I'M GETTING CROTCHETY, BUT sometimes it seems there's a plague of unnecessary noise out there.

Here's the scene. I'm snug in my porch hammock, indulging in a good mystery and perhaps a snooze. I swing, peacefully. Cardinals call; flowering annuals beckon to butterflies drifting by on the light breeze. But then the deep thump-thump of a car's stereo super woofers vibrates my bones and dental fillings. My mood changes to profound annoyance. The car, instinctively knowing how this sound can irritate, takes its time moving down the street; residents are thoroughly enveloped in that pulsing, basso profundo throb. Attached to his cell phone, the driver is oblivious to my disgruntled glare. How, I wonder, can he, or the party to whom he is speaking, hear themselves think?

A while back I happened upon the Discovery Channel's exposé of the sex life of the American prairie chicken. It seems that amorous, unattached males stake out territory and then defend it with massively expanded chests, which produce the same throbbing sound! I was astounded and amused. Young, hopeful, unmarried human males transmit eerily similar signals, from their territory, the car. The only mystery is, who has copied whom? Even more intriguing: will this thumpety-bump attract available young females?

Finally the throb dissipates. But now the irritating whine of a leaf blower fractures the peace; a bored young fellow wields it, dedicated to chasing every unattached leaf and twig straight into the gutter. He swings the blower rhythmically, chewing gum at a rapid rate; agitated debris rises every which way. The noise causes my neighbor to shout his front-porch conversation with friends. The assault goes on for an interminable time; when the wretched machine finally stops whining, the silence is shocking. The birds wait to tune up; it would be a cheep waste of breath.

I listen intently: is he finally finished? Quiet reigns, and I settle back and pick up where the chief inspector is sipping bad coffee and evaluating the evidence. With a little poke from my foot the hammock gently swings. Bliss.

AWK! The roar of a big power mower splits the air, and I sit bolt upright, staring wildly at this new sound, furious that it signifies nothing but misery for at least fifteen minutes more. I wince as the fellow whizzes by a young tree in full throttle, grazing the bark. Sigh…whatever happened to push-mowers, and the friendly murmur of whirring blades?

Eventually the roar stops with a cough. Again, quiet creeps back, but warily this time. The sun is lower now, and the steady whap-whap of tires on brick tells me the workday is ending; dinner and family lure workers home. Almost all hold one ear as they drive by, and their mouths move.

Hoping for peace, I decide to count to a hundred. If there were no new attack by then, it would probably be safe to resume my attempts to discover whodunit. I get as far as sixty-two, when a thousand angry hornets vocalize at once. Wearily, I peer over my book. Yep. It's a weed whacker, busily decapitating everything in its path.

This can't last. I mutter hopefully, "He's almost done. Hang on...."

Abrupt silence. The whacker's packed up. There's a fractional pause. The truck door slams shut. Its engine starts.... YES! He's gone!

Ahhh. The evening is lovely. I savor the stillness, swing gently, and turn the page, as tentative chirping resumes...

Suddenly, there's a high-pitched whiiiine! ARGHHH! With a groan, I smack my arm. The mosquitoes have arrived!

Stunning Vistas, Gargoyle Thoughts

IT'S A GORGEOUS AFTERNOON. I'M sitting on a stone bench under a magnificent shade tree, whose leafy arms hover protectively over visitors. In front of me a large, lily-padded pond hosts darting red carp; lush, clumped grasses seem content to be partially submerged. This place is in the heart of the University of Chicago's quadrangle, which is surrounded by wonderful, gargoyle-infested stone buildings designed in the classic Cambridge tradition, and funded by the vast Rockefeller fortune.

The thick, closely mown grass gleams in dappled sunlight; all around me are well-tended flowerbeds, where the beautiful frosted leaves of dead nettle (*Lamium*) and the green fronds of exhausted daylilies still manage to charm—no stalks poke unattractively through the foliage. Asters bloom profusely near the water, their cheerful blue faces basking in the late afternoon sun. Pig-squeak (*Bergenia*) lines the small path leading to a bridge over calm water; fat, vocal frogs regularly penetrate its surface. Close by, huge black-iron fences, supported by seven-foot stone pillars, add dimension to this stunning vista. The park-like quad behind me boasts immense, towering trees, still richly green. Boston ivy thickly blankets the buildings, effortlessly climbing six stories, leaving only windows free; its foliage hints at the red show to come.

A snarl of bicycles parked across the wide pedestrian walk is near two ornate, fifteen-foot high, black-iron gates built under a giant stone archway that marks the boundary of the quadrangle. Half the gate invites souls to pass through; the other half is closed, exhibiting its classic lines. Ten fearsome gargoyles perch menacingly atop that structure; their eyes glare, as if daring us to Step From The Path. Three of these wondrous beasts are big as horses; all are unique. The smaller ones, teeth bared, writhe sinuously as they follow our movements. Their huge talons are anchored in stone; they'll be there long after we're gone.

People hurry by, dragging their thoughts along, anxious to be where they are not; most carry paper-packed briefcases that jostle their arms and legs and remind each harried soul that soon enough that intellectual weight must be absorbed.

There is a kind of peace here; city noise is absent, and I relax into reverie.

What is it about a university that moves me toward meditation?

Perhaps it's a sub-surface intensity radiating from people who are part of it—separate universes of random, tangled thoughts trying to organize to change not only their own personal operating manual, but also the world's. (Friedman, Sagan, Hubbell, and Russell come to mind.) Knowledge cements the stones in university buildings; its collective power supports these dreaming spires, which offer an intellectual haven, a sanctuary, from the rough weather of ignorance. One could not flourish without the other.

Perhaps it's the wonderful architecture, so reminiscent of the Old World from which Rockefeller took his inspiration. Here is a physical connection to our collective pasts, and to the ideas that gave birth to revolutions. These reassuring monoliths radiate a heavy power, tempered by the cloister of loveliness within their walls, where gardens like this serve as a balm for the soul. They are places to get clean, to move closer to the earth, to remind ourselves that we will be part of its ancient wisdom soon enough.

The wind ruffles my hair, breaking my reverie, reminding me that I must soon pass under the watchful gate guardians and move about the ordinary world, where bellies and cars need filling, and practical thoughts elbow their way in.

For just a little longer, though, I gaze, ponder, and smile.

From Terror to Triumph: A Man and His Music

TV IS A MERCILESS MEDIUM. Almost everyone is familiar with shows that feature amateur talent: a contestant trots out there and tries to dazzle everyone with, say, swallowing an ostrich effortlessly. His five minutes of fame ends in a burp. He's either done, or done in by sarcastic judges. Or, if the audience likes his shtick, he may be chosen to remain in competition.

I've never been able to sit through even one. They're probably interesting; contestants are often talented, but their vulnerability to the judges' acid commentaries makes me cringe.

And yet... A friend emailed me a British video of a national talent competition I'll never forget.

The three judges, bored (though they tried to hide it), sat rapping their pencils while a tallish, neatly dressed fellow, introduced as Paul, walked uncertainly out under the hot lights. He was thirtysomething, slightly overweight, and frightened. At one point he looked about to cry. But he stood his ground.

"What are you here for?" asked the elegant female judge.

"I'll sing opera," Paul replied softly. There was a distinct "Oh, no, spare me" look from the male judges, while the woman fought to keep her face carefully neutral. The audience waited.

He collected himself and nodded to the technician on the sidelines, who began the recorded orchestral introduction. As his entrance approached, something incredible happened. Falling headlong into the aria, he forgot everything but the music. The man sang! There were no planned gestures, and no theatrics; he really didn't move, but his hands, held quietly at his sides, opened slightly, and his brown eyes shone as, with perfect intonation and astonishing breath control, he delivered each wonderful note.

The judges sat frozen, eyes wide, mouths agape, pencils stilled, not believing their ears. The audience exploded, cheering, unable to help themselves, giving Paul new courage just when he needed it, because the most demanding vocal part was yet to come. His marvelous voice soared effortlessly above the huge crowd with perfect control, as he poured everything he had into his passion. The orchestra carried him to the climax of that glorious aria...and then the music gently subsided. He stood alone out there quietly, a Presence now. A tremulous smile emerged as the audience went wild, standing, whistling, screaming, and clapping their hands raw. Many people, including the female judge, sat back, stunned, wiping away tears, trying to absorb what had happened. They finally joined in the applause, smiling and shaking their heads, awed.

He'd done it. He had overcome a lifetime of shy diffidence and dared to follow his dream. Welshmen are renowned for their singing. But this very private man had submerged his talent, struggling instead to earn a modest living selling mobile phones.

Somehow, he'd summoned the courage to enter this national competition, his love for "what I was born to do" blazing through his fear. It was surely an Awakening, and possibly the greatest moment of his life.

The judges gave unequivocal "yes" votes, after glowing comments, predicting he'd go far. Paul Potts bowed, nodding thanks; his shy, thrilled smile wrenched my heart. He left the stage to handshakes all around from the backstage crew, as the audience, obviously reluctant to let him go, continued to clap and cheer.

That three-minute concert was, for me, a world-class musical Moment.

Surely, Someone Important will contact him.

Surely.

Postscript: Paul Potts is now an international sensation, touring Europe and earning millions of pounds as a singer. My daughter gifted me that Christmas with his exquisite debut CD.

A Swinging Hotel for Feline Phantoms

ONE MORNING, AFTER ENJOYING AROMATIC Kenya coffee and crunchy bacon, I opened the front door and walked out into the crisp air. It was dark, even at 7:00 A.M. Idly, I strolled to the side of the porch. Which triggered annoyed exclamations, and soft, multiple thumps! The porch swing rocked; indistinct forms shot away from the wicker furniture and vanished into the night.

Startled, I grabbed the railing. I felt the plump seat cushions; all were warm. Raccoons? Nah. Those fatties would lumber off. This, I realized, was a cattery. The creatures had created their own hotel; not only were the comfortable chairs sheltered from wind and rain, but also their location offered a fine view of prey that might be careless enough to poke around that spot for bugs and worms. They'd be pre-heated hors d'oeuvres for this cadre of cats.

Wait a minute! I vaguely recalled noticing three rumpled feathers at the first gate. Now I understood: These hunters had killed and eaten a careless mallard, discarding only the quack. So many felines would make short work of any curious duck keen to dine on my lush Irish moss (and the bugs bunked underneath).

Come to think of it, rabbit poop, too, had been absent from the garden for quite a while.

How long, I mused, had this been a hotel for hunters? They'd cannily taken care not to claw the cushions. I often swung there, and would have noticed that my furniture was doubling as bed. These practical cats had probably agreed to keep their daggers sheathed. It wasn't sensible to provoke the proprietor.

I think I know why the "hotel" got started.

Last season, robins had built a nest high atop the clematis trellis that framed this first part of the garden. I found that curious. Why hadn't they chosen the eighty-foot blue spruce next to it? Perhaps they thought a clear view was safer. Various cats had made numerous attempts to ascend that vertical face, but it had proven too daunting. They'd found themselves entangled in an impenetrable thicket of crisscrossing vines, and effectively blinded by billions of blanketing leaves. The frantic father bird, constantly aware of how close the cat-of-the-day was, would scream insults and dive at unprotected feline rear ends, no doubt praying that vine-y obstacles would prove he'd chosen right.

It must have been a harrowing six weeks. When the kids were finally fledged, the exhausted male robin must have opted for a vasectomy.

Denied airborne prey, the frustrated cats had opted to hunt closer to the ground.

I've named them. Soprano had come to the door weeks earlier, meowing insistently for admittance for an hour, mystifying me; he'd finally stalked off, disgusted. Rip-Torn (ragged ears), Fergie (don't ask), Bent (tail pokes oddly), and occasionally,

Potbelly (might have a family to feed soon) make up the rest of this motley crew. Nobody turns down cushy beds, a great view, and fresh hot meals. My bed-and-breakfast nook, situated so conveniently amid ducky natural attractions, has proven irresistible.

Poetry in Motion: Toronto Horse Magic

NOT LONG AGO MY HUSBAND told me to pack my passport and warm clothes. We'd have a three-day adventure!

So we boarded a roomy tour bus at 6:00 A.M. in Saginaw, bound for Toronto. Only then did Joe reveal our destination—the Royal Agricultural Show, followed by the Royal Horse Show. I was astounded and intrigued. Decades ago I'd wanted to be a jockey. Small, agile, and empathic, I'd handled difficult horses easily, even very young. Alas, mid-puberty trotted out severe allergies; that dream was tearfully abandoned.

It was pleasant to glide along; we read, slept, and inspected silly merchandise at various dreary Canadian pit stops.

Nine hours later thirty bus-weary people arrived in downtown Toronto, only to be enveloped in a massive traffic jam: some idiot had boxed an old-fashioned alarm clock, then placed it inside a bank near our destination, the elegant Royal York Hotel. The "bomb" was eventually exposed as a hoax, but two extra hours in the bus made bottoms and tempers raw.

On Saturday the excited group was trundled in that bus to the immense indoor arena. We blended into the huge crowd, eager to inspect hundreds of booths crammed with fascinating animal paraphernalia, from tooth-filers for cows to Spock-like earmuffs for horses. Amid the delicious smells of leather, pizza, hay, and warm beasts, judges inspected beautifully groomed, bored milk-cows. In another smallish ring an American Standardbred colt strutted nervously around on a lead, his silky gait admired by hordes of fascinated children pressed against the makeshift corral. We admired artists as they effortlessly created lifelike portraits of horses from photographs; we inspected jewelry, saddles and horsebox-trailers with attached bedrooms. Women with stiff blue and purple hair, wearing heavy leather chaps and acres of fringe, chewed gum while discussing their various cowponies...

Finally, 7:00 P.M. arrived. The crowd settled down for the sold-out show.

We gasped at the giant Shire and Percheron horse teams dragging heavy dray carts. Their elegantly clad drivers made controlling twelve thousand pounds of power look easy. Many had come from impossibly distant countries to compete for first prize. (Only the super-rich could afford this hobby.)

We goggled at ponies who pulled four-wheeled carts; each perfect animal pranced enthusiastically in front of impassive judges, knees nearly touching noses. I was dumbstruck.

We gaped at eighteen glittering cowgirls trailing Canadian flags, riding complicated Esther Williams routines; we watched nervously as a ballerina danced daintily on a trotting horse's broad, white back. Coveted prizes were duly awarded amid appreciative applause.

The lights dimmed. A slim woman riding a huge, beautiful horse would now demonstrate freestyle dressage, as a treat. Jacqueline

Brooks and Gran Gesto, her horse, had won the world's top prize that afternoon.

Ten thousand people went silent. The horse waited, calmly. Commanding orchestral music began.

Oh! It was incredible! Long tail swishing, he glided effortlessly around the marked demonstration space, changing leads, trotting sideways, trotting in place, !skipping!, moving smoothly to the music, changing from one schooled step to the next, flawlessly. With nothing left to win, they thoroughly enjoyed themselves.

Tears fell: I would have crawled to Toronto to see this.

They finished to thunderous applause. Gran Gesto skipped out, neck arched, knowing he was Best Beast. His proud rider beamed. I sat, paralyzed. I'd witnessed poetry in motion: years of discipline had culminated in mastery of this marvelous, demanding art.

Next, twenty-four of the world's best jumpers competed for mega-prizes by soaring over impossible fences in under seventy seconds. I hardly noticed. I was still reliving that miraculous five minutes of dressage. At midnight we staggered to the bus, mute.

The bus traveled home the next day, carrying a very different Dee from the one who had ridden to Toronto. I felt changed by what I'd seen. The memory of that perfection still brings me to tears.

Stealthy Home Invaders

I KEEP A NEAT HOUSE. Nooks and crannies are free of dust bunnies, floors are swept, carpeted are vacuumed regularly, and dishes washed and dried. But still, I face pesky challenges.

Recently I staggered in from raking leaves. I was starved. I washed up, preheated the oven, and prepared two chicken legs for my daily meal. While they baked, I found the movie channel—yay! *Arsenic and Old Lace* always sends me into fits of laughter.

Eventually the chicken was done. I placed the meat and some veggies on my plate, then returned to Cary's dilemma. Dinner could wait a minute; Grant's aunts had stored another body in the window seat.

Suddenly, a movement caught my eye. I tore myself away from screen silliness, glancing instinctively toward my food. There, sitting on his haunches amid my veggies, was a mouse, cradling one warm chicken leg, munching on it happily. He'd actually turned his back to me, feeling unthreatened. I gaped, paralyzed with shock. HOW COULD THIS HAPPEN?

The mouse, realizing he'd been "made," looked at me reproachfully. Then, sighing, he reluctantly set the leg aside, and, after daintily brushing peas off his bottom, stepped nimbly off the plate and vanished down the stove burners.

I was speechless. A rodent had ruined my dinner! Right in front of me! The brazenness of it blew me away. Aren't mice supposed to be shy??

Yeah, right. He was four feet away, acting like a guest. Truly, I wouldn't have been surprised to see a napkin tucked under his non-existent chin.

With tears of rage I threw out the chicken, grabbed my wallet, and ran to Ace Hardware, where I purchased a Hav-a-Hart mousetrap. Why this sort?

Well, poison would work, but it takes a while, and then the smell from the dead mouse, who'd hide in the walls, is awful for weeks. A traditional trap meant facing a corpse in the kitchen. Like Grant, I found killing even this bold home invader to be too much. The only other option was to live-trap. Groan...Gritting my teeth I shelled out twenty dollars, then bought cheap processed cheese, and thumped back home, stomach growling.

For two days I found the trap tripped, and the cheese gone. Huh. This was no ordinary foe. But I was surely smarter than one sassy rodent. So I had a think. I'd set the trap to remain open. He'd nibble the cheese without incident; eventually, he'd get complacent. Then I'd have him.

I padded downstairs the fourth day to find him rattling the bars, clearly frustrated. He'd gotten cocky, imbibed, and SLAM! Gleeful, I let him fume there while I leisurely drank my coffee and read the paper. Sweet revenge.

Eventually I popped the trap into a large grocery bag—I couldn't let the neighbors see, now could I?—and padded to the Union Street Bridge. The mini-forest surrounding was obvious mouse territory. I climbed down the worn, dark, dirt path toward the water, and carefully opened the trap door. After a disbelieving moment, the mouse ventured out, tossed me a disdainful glance, and zipped into the foliage.

Triumphantly I ambled home, but the icy air prompted another disconcerting thought. Where there's one mouse, there are others. Mice make more mice at an astounding rate.

EEK!

I quickly caught two more; one was a baby. After that, I've been mouse-free. Perhaps life in Hannah Park, across the street, had been difficult, so this enterprising rodent family had stealthily invaded my home, feeling themselves much safer.

HA! Wanna bet?

An Unforgettable Cat Tale

ANIMALS ARE INCREDIBLY RESILIENT. I saw a cat the other day, walking quietly on a leash with her owner, not seeming to mind the snowy scene. This pussy, rescued from a cruel situation, was mending in a loving home. Her sleek marmalade coat reminded me of Jinjii-cat, who lived the first five years of her long life on the Isle of Skye, in a snug country cottage with my mother and her beloved husband, David.

Jinjii, an attractive tortoiseshell kitty, was friendly but independent, preferring to live outside most of the time. As David puts it,

"I always gave her the choice. Before I locked up for the night I'd hold the door open. If she wanted out, she went; if not, she'd spend the night in her bed in the kitchen."

She loved to wind around their legs, answering their questions with meows. Jinjii would often bring them gifts, like horrified, wriggling rabbits or dead mice, and occasionally even birds, which she'd deposit at their feet, looking pleased with herself.

One Sunday morning, though, when Jinjii was about three, David got a terrible shock. When he opened the door to let her in for breakfast and a fireside snooze, he found her sitting quietly on the stoop, looking up at him. She held out her front leg, like an offering, too exhausted to meow. Clamped firmly to her small paw, which seemed to be nearly severed, was a huge steel trap, complete with heavy chain. The whole thing weighed about four pounds. It must have been unthinkably painful to stagger over that wild terrain to her home, dragging the trap and chain.

My mother held her while David gently pried the hideous jaws open. Jinjii, her eyes closed, allowed this. In a remarkable demonstration of her trust in them, she briefly purred.

"We drove her into the little village of Portree," David recalls, "and woke the vet, who carefully examined her. The skin was broken; her paw was crushed. His advice was to trust to nature. We took her home and put her to bed, where she fell deeply asleep for two days. On the third day she weakly asked to go outside, where she somehow managed to scrape a hole and do her business, cover it, then hobble back to bed. For weeks, except for brief, painful visits to the garden, she would sleep, eat a bit, and lap milk. During this time I wrote a letter to the local newspaper offering to return the trap to its owner, firmly attached to a certain part of his anatomy. No one claimed it; the police took it away.

"Although it was illegal, some crofters would fix these traps to fencepost tops to catch the hated 'hoodies'—hooded crows that prey on newborn lambs.

"As the weeks went by Jinjii tentatively put her leg to the ground; after about four months, she could walk on it. After five months she could extend and retract her claws. She began spending more time outside. With her claws ready for action, we felt she was as good as new."

Eventually, in 1981, they all moved to the west of England to our present country home, Bryn Garth Cottage.

There, for the next fourteen years, unaffected by her terrible ordeal, Jinjii thrived, along with the family dog Kate (who has her own amazing story). Finally, at age nineteen, she died in David's arms.

He puts it best: "Her life was idyllic; she was cared for, but never pampered, and given perfect freedom to be a cat."

Lucky Jinjii.

An Alley Explorer's Adventure

THE WORLD IS WEDDING-CAKE white. As usual, I delight in winter. Though the season is young, the city's already been thumped by four inches of snow, then a thick ice slice, topped by more snow—a formidable sandwich. Shifting it has been quite a job. Two strong young men with shovels keep my driveway and garage accessible.

As I crunched out to admire their efforts and dump trash, a very big, glossy black four-door sedan, with a very small, warmly-bundled elderly lady at the wheel crept down the alley and, with great deliberation, stopped next to me. The car was put carefully into "park." Then, after a small search, the woman located, and pressed, a button. Soundlessly the window lowered, and she leaned toward me, politely. There was an opened city map on the seat. "Hello, dear. Can you reassure me that I'm heading for Munson Hospital?"

Before I could respond, she continued, in proper Victorian diction. "There is one thing: please direct me via the alley system. I try to avoid busy streets, as I don't always have enough time to make decisions. People are whizzing about, impatient, wanting me to move faster. These alleys are much more peaceful—and interesting. I can go slowly; no one minds. In fact, residents wave their thanks. Traverse City has a wonderful network of alleys that I suspect are under-appreciated as throughways for the slower set."

Huh. Fascinating thought. I'd never considered alleys in this way before.

She went on. "I'm eager to arrive there; I'd love to manage it before one o'clock."

Oh, no. Was someone very ill, and perhaps scheduled for surgery? She did look slightly anxious.

I leaned in, and explained that she could continue as she was going, since the alley opened onto Division. From there she could cross, then continue along a fairly quiet Sixth Street until she saw the hospital. It would be impossible to miss.

Looking pleased, she made minute adjustments to the mirror, straightened her hat and said,

"I don't travel to faraway places anymore; I'm too old. But I still love mini-adventures. Alley exploration exactly suits me. I see things people miss: cats, and dogs with coats—one lady had fashioned boots for her dog, Hector." She laughed at that name choice. "Parents pull children on bright sleds. My father used to do that with me. Plus, I view old homes from an entirely different perspective." Her face lit up. "Once, I saw a fox crossing! One Sunday, quite early, a raccoon family stopped to let me pass; they'd been inspecting garbage cans. That was a while ago…it gave me the idea for these little adventures. I use hardly any gas, and Tom's happy the car is driven."

Seeing my interest, she carried on. "My grandson gave me Tank—he calls this car a tank because it's so solid—to use for my forays. It is a comfort, I confess."

She looked at me, her eyes shining, and said, "I'm ninety years young, still curious, still able. Today I've planned a visit to the hospital's cafeteria for a light lunch. My friend recommends their lemon meringue pie. But I mustn't arrive after one o'clock; pie pieces vanish. I still have plenty of time, though."

She told me she constantly pondered the reality of never being sure of living through each fresh day. She felt fine, mind you, and her mother had lived to nearly a hundred, then simply popped off in the middle of sipping strong coffee. She mused aloud that if her maker were to take her this afternoon, she would conveniently be at the hospital, and thus cause little fuss. It would, she speculated, be a neat and tidy passing.

"It's such a nice day for an 'alley-venture;' I usually wind up in interesting places. Merry Christmas!"

She smiled her thanks, rolled up the window, adjusted the pillows under her, put the car in gear, and rolled slowly away, her head swiveling back and forth, making sure she missed nothing.

Who says ninety is old?

A 2008 Makeover:

Tweaking Me

RECENTLY I SAW MY REFLECTION in a full-length mirror, and decided then and there that a makeover might be a good idea. Some firm promises were made to the rumpled, poke-haired image gazing back at me.

My family has noted that I've rediscovered perfume, abandoned for fifteen years because the bees were stung when I didn't live up to my flowery promise—I'd frequently felt their displeasure. My husband would hint, leaving delightful sample vials where I couldn't miss them, but insect-opinions mattered more. Fortunately, his patience has paid off. I'll indulge in this delight for half of every year, with no penalty.

Reluctantly, I've stopped cutting my own hair. For thirty-six years I'd managed this task well, enjoying the challenge, as well as the often-interesting result. But finally it's proved too much. I lost an eye five years ago in a near-fatal auto accident, and when I tried to artistically trim and shape with just the one, all I got for my trouble were multi-snipped hands, and a weirdly jagged, lopsided topknot, stained red. Obstinate, I persisted for a long time, hoping I'd get the hang of it, but finally, defeated, I slunk off to a proper salon nearby to see what could be resurrected. Hanks of hair poked here and there; clearly I'd simply chopped off the bits that had blocked my view of important gardeny things.

My hairdresser had to have been horrified; I looked like something the cat rejected. But noticing my nervousness, she'd cheerfully chatted about how to proceed. Armed with old photos and a sketch, her clever scissor-hands snipped and shaped. Good heavens! I realized I'd been gone a long time.

Inspired, I'm looking hard at clothes I kept for years. After bagging most for Goodwill, I've rediscovered some classics that still fit nicely. Out of practice, I sometimes emerge from furtive dress-up sessions piecemeal, but mostly, I'm feminine again—for six months.

I've resolved to change my watchband before it resembles Shredded Wheat.

There are limits. I'll never care about nails, jewelry or make-up. I won't dangle my glasses from strings; they'll always park precariously on my head. I'll continue to cherish cargo pants, attracted by the many pockets I can stuff with pruners, twine, Velcro, plant labels and Kleenex. (I'm lumpy in the oddest places...) And I'll don whatever footgear feels wonderful. I have large feet; many years ago I wisely decided that accommodating them meant I'd always have good balance. (High heels and I are natural enemies.)

When I was a pig-tailed thirteen, and horse-crazy, I gleefully purchased (with a year's saved babysitting money) roomy, pointy-toed, ornately tooled black cowboy boots. A western store downtown, three bus stops away, sold them, along with other ranch-style gear. Though wonderfully comfortable they looked ridiculous, overwhelming my five-foot tall, 110-pound frame finished by size eight-and-a-half feet.

But I saw what I wanted to see. When I clumped into the kitchen to show them off, my shocked mother, tactful but firm, hustled me into the car. We returned them as she firmly chastised the bewildered clerk. Thus my Dale Evans look died at birth; I settled for saddle shoes.

Today, still a twitch over five feet tall, but less rumpled, wafting faint perfume and reasonably shod, I'll stride confidently into this fresh new year. I have a renewed appreciation of how lucky I am to be alive. Taking better care of my body seemed like a good way to celebrate.

Beetles, Lice and Long Memories

HERE I STAND, PEERING INTO a pot, waiting for inspiration. Sometimes, for fun, I'll rummage through the pantry extracting stuff stored there, like whole-wheat pasta, a forgotten jar of artichoke hearts, dried soup ingredients, interesting sauces, or microscopically inspected rice. (More on that, later.) I'll mix it all together with minced beef, season, and sample the result, which might be delicious, or head-cocked odd—or I might furtively visit the garbage disposal to obliterate whatever had offended my long-suffering taste buds. (I used to give larger culinary failures a secret burial in the garden.)

My mother, a marvelous cook, would spend hours baking, or preparing fine, artistic meals. She mourned my stubborn ignorance.

As an undergrad, I'd run the mile to the sorority house between classes to eat what I'd already paid for. In grad school, apartment "cooking" meant toasted ham and cheese, or peanut butter, banana and mayo sandwiches, devoured on the fly.

These days I get a kick out of knocking meals together with whatever happens to be around. Occasionally, though, aliens lurk amid the ingredients.

My kitchen aversion began with a beetle. One April morning when I was twelve, I tucked into corn flakes that were topped with bright raspberries that my mother had handpicked and frozen the previous autumn. These beauties were huge and absolutely delicious.

As I aimed the loaded spoon at my mouth, a dark movement caught my eye. I froze, then watched in horror as a huge black beetle, antennae waving, sleepily emerged from its plump red berry-nest. Its tidily folded wings began to twitch, experimentally. (Though frozen for months, it had revived in the warm kitchen.)

The shock of that discovery, and the realization of what I'd almost devoured, defies description. I screamed, threw the poor beast—still riding the milky spoon—across the breakfast table, and ran to the bathroom.

Kitchens, which already represented dirty dishes and tables that constantly required setting or dismantling, were now connected in my mind to horrific surprises. Twelve is an intense, impressionable age: one inoffensive beetle's dramatic entrance made an indelible imprint on me. Thirteen more years would pass before culinary curiosity overcame my aversion.

(Amusingly, that same dramatic "freak-out" was regularly practiced on me. Pre-pubescent schoolboys thumping baseball mitts would react to this "tweeny" girl's sudden appearance with horror, theatrically gagging before running away in disgust. I bugged them. Too young then to grasp the irony, I felt no empathy for the beetle.)

My mother commented once that whenever God was bored He'd entertain himself in, er, creative ways: beetles, berries, breakfast, and budding teens made for great spontaneous theatre.

Time passed. Just when Mom dared to hope that my one-trial learning wasn't permanent, rice lice appeared in my cooking pot. Observing these minute, multi-legged creatures trying to escape drowning by climbing onto floating kernels of (long-expired) rice firmly reinforced my "cookaphobia." Not that these fears were rational. In my twenties I, much like flat-tasting, unsimmered soup, required seasoning and time to enhance my anorexic critical thinking skills. "Insects" and "kitchens" were (almost) anagrams: college men, like bugs, had too many arms. Sigh…life was incredibly confusing.)

Anyway, forty happy years later, Joe and I rarely bug each other. I've mastered the finer points of fashioning simple, nourishing fare, with flair. But I still approach raspberries with caution. Though beetle-thoughts no longer unduly influence my enjoyment, this fruit, designed with holes, still makes assembling certain desserts slow going, since I'm compelled to peek into every opening. And yeah, other innocent foods may sometimes endure a surprise inspection as well.

(I found a worm in the lettuce once…)

Canine Wish: "Let It Rain! Let It Pour!"

ONE WET DAY, I GRABBED my biggest umbrella and strolled to Hannah Park, just across the street. Every so often I'll get the urge to walk in the rain. It didn't hurt that I'd just enjoyed watching Gene Kelly make dance-magic in a downpour; I wanted to recapture his exuberance for a while. My day had been bumpy, but gazing at the Boardman River, dotted with delighted vocal ducks, always lifts my spirits.

I carefully descended the steep cement stairs to the river—and came upon an amazing sight. A large golden retriever stood squarely in the middle of the meadow, eyes closed, legs spread out, paws splayed, head slightly raised, and utterly transported. The rain was pouring buckets. Even the ducks had sought shelter under one of the big trees. But that dog, drenched to the skin, had planted himself there, willing it to fall even harder; the wetter he got, the better. His fur actually parted in the middle from the weight of the water.

His owner, decked out in rain gear, waited patiently under a tree. He noticed me watching his dog, and chuckled. "Sailor lives for these times. He does his rounds, then finds the perfect spot and places himself like that. Odd, eh? He's too old to manage the river, it moves pretty fast; so he gets his fix this way. I think the experience must be similar to a massage."

"Sailor? What a great name!"

The man sighed. "Yeah; when my wife and I brought him home (he was ten weeks old) we noticed he took a great interest in the kitchen faucets. Then, when she decided to take a shower, and turned it on, Sailor was riveted! He yipped, then hopped in and began snapping at the spray, inspecting the drain, and generally making himself at home. Eventually he just stood there, in the same position he's in now, and let himself get pummeled. I swear that pup smiled. We knew then what to call him."

I looked carefully. Sailor hadn't moved. And, by golly, he was smiling. That dog was the picture of contentment.

"He's lucky we're willing to indulge this. It's rarely convenient for my wife and me to walk him in torrential rain, but we're always rewarded."

For nearly ten minutes we enjoyed his enjoyment. Chatting and laughing, raising our voices to accommodate the downpour, we swapped dog stories. Sailor was nine. They'd adopted him from an animal shelter in Wisconsin, where they lived. The couple had seen their daughter off to college, but within two months began suffering an acute case of empty nest syndrome. Sailor was their cure.

The rain lessened. It was time to break the spell. The man whistled and shook the leash. "Wrap it up, partner!"

Reluctantly Sailor opened his eyes, gave a heartfelt sigh, and shook himself mightily. A ton of water flew every which way. Two more vigorous shakes, and they squelched over to a blue van. After a thorough toweling, Sailor hopped onto the tarped front passenger seat, accepted a large Milk-Bone, and dispatched it with relish. "We bought a heck of a hair dryer when the house started to reek of sopping canine. Making him acceptable takes time, but it's necessary. He settles down to wait for rain; when he dreams, it's not about squirrels, believe me."

A cheerful wave, and they were off to join his wife. Sailor sat, sodden and happy. Obviously this was a familiar routine.

I sloshed home, grinning in the rain.

More On Sailor, An Old Seadog

IN MY LAST COLUMN I narrated the soaking saga of Sailor, an old golden retriever who loved drenching rains. His owner had told his story for years with resignation and humor. His wife and he had learned to enjoy downpours, but, to Sailor's dismay, they could never be persuaded to go out when there was thunder. The dog eventually learned that there was rain—and thunder-rain. He'd always ask anyway, for form's sake, but knew that thunder-rain would always mean disappointment.

I told him about our Golden, Buck, who died thirteen years ago. The minute we released him, he would throw himself ecstatically into the Boardman River. He loved to paddle around in circles, barking with pleasure, or float downstream for a bit, or, best of all, swim vigorously after tossed sticks. His most interesting talent, though, was to dive for stones. If finding the correct one proved impossible, he'd swim closer to shore, his head making sweeping motions under water, searching for stones to drag ashore. Failure to retrieve was not an option. Buck could stay under for quite a while, and never minded getting water up his considerable nose. When it was finally time to go home, he, like Sailor, would whine, then shake himself resignedly, while tossing us looks of deep disappointment.

Heaven for both dogs was near-total immersion, and as often as possible.

(Every winter Sailor had to be carefully watched. He might walk too far out, fall through thin lake ice and freeze to death, unable to extract himself.)

They'd never taken him out for a boat ride, afraid he'd leap overboard, and prove impossible to hoist back. (Wet, large, long-haired canines are incredibly heavy to heave.) So, he stayed home. It was best, his owner mused, not to tempt fate.

Good call.

Uh-Oh! Foot-Draggers Stalk Grand Opera

OPERA CAN BE WONDERFUL—AND full of surprises.

One day, downtown, I overheard a woman who was determined to administer "enrichment" to her protesting husband. "Our reborn State Theatre," she said, "is bringing us live opera, right here in Traverse City, straight from New York's Metropolitan Opera House. Try it, this once."

Hmmm, I thought, perhaps many "significant others" are dragged into that elegant darkness, muttering that opera isn't really their thing.

Though the sets are usually spectacular, reluctant viewers, faced with three hours of incomprehensible Italian shouted by giant-lunged tenors and equally chesty sopranos, may conclude that's all there is. During intermission they'll huddle with other like-minded souls who long for a touch of Kiss, or even Gordon Lightfoot.

But take heart! There is a way to make this experience suspenseful. Sit quietly and wait, because a major operatic "oops" might make your day.

These performances are live. Remember live TV in the old days? They had to get it right the first time. Even steel-nerved pros could be unraveled by embarrassing, outrageous showbiz disasters.

With opera, the beleaguered management routinely deals with complicated sets, multiple exotic animals, unpredictable machinery, and scenes involving fire, water, and battles. Combined with singers' massive egos, sudden memory lapses and suchlike, this brew is potentially explosive. Anything can happen.

For example:

Puccini's *Tosca*, sung in New York in the sixties, starred an imperious soprano who was thoroughly disliked by the stage crew. They allowed the opera to proceed uneventfully until the climax, when, with her cry, *"Scarpia, davanti a Dio!"* the diva hurled herself off the castle battlements—but didn't meet the customary thick mattress, for a huge trampoline had been substituted. To the audience's delight she bounced up numerous times, shouting with maniacal laughter and rage, before the curtain mercifully fell. San Francisco became her base for a long time after that—East Coast patrons' memories were long.

Once, during Mozart's *Don Giovanni* at the Vienna State Opera, when the tenor star descended to Hell's nether regions amid smoke and thunder, the stage lift stuck halfway down, leaving his upper body exposed. Keeping his head, he signaled that they should try again to lower him; alas, the same thing happened. Instead of crumbling, the indomitable tenor, amid the audience's horrified silence, sang, in Italian, "Oh my God, how wonderful—Hell is full!" The applause was deafening.

In another *Don Giovanni* in New York, a technical hitch of a kind that haunts stage managers came to pass. For ten seconds, eighteenth-century Spain became East Fifty-Fifth Street, with honking cabs, whizzing cars and amazed cops. The vast backstage doors had mistakenly been opened as the crew switched sets.

Once, during *Boris Gudonov* at the Royal Opera House in Covent Garden, a truly epic-sized tenor, playing a heroic army commander, sat uncertainly on a giant, compliant horse, which only just managed to support him. The animal stood patiently while the guy sang his inspiring aria, but, during the applause, it offered its own impressive contribution. Then another poor soul had to sing of the ruin of Russia immediately afterward, amid the steaming pile of poop.

Finally, during Verdi's *Rigoletto*, in Paris, the worst happened. When emotions were at their height, Rigoletto's huge hump gradually slid down his back and parked itself prominently on his bottom. The baritone's frantic, vain efforts to raise it while singing brought down the house.

Maybe now you won't balk. Go with grace, and pay attention. With luck you could catch 'em in the act. Finding Grand Opera *in flagrante delicto* is worth the wait.

Note: These examples were taken from *Great Operatic Disasters*, by Hugh Vickers (St. Martin's Press, 1979).

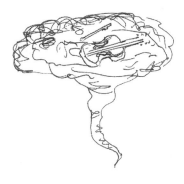

More Opera Shenanigans

OPERA'S EXCEPTIONAL SINGERS REACH to impossible heights with perfectly placed, exquisite high notes, which leave audiences trembling with awe. Puccini's *Madame Butterfly*, my favorite, offers a classic wartime story, combined with achingly lovely arias that always make me cry.

But, for those less enthusiastic patrons, a night at the opera can still be interesting. Even if you're not the least bit musical, you'll certainly wallow in extravagance. The scenery alone is usually arresting. (And, to add to the spectacle, it might be wobbly, or reluctant to cooperate.)

In my last column I gave some funny examples of what can happen. Some of these situations made the *Ann Arbor News* when I was a college student. I remember chuckling over the plight of famous singers who found themselves the victims of outrageous fortune, or their own haughtiness.

Not all divas are difficult. Plump, red-haired Beverly Sills was loved by the Met. Affectionately known as "Bubbles" because of her effervescent personality, she delighted audiences with her glorious voice and ready smiles. Her eventual retirement saddened everybody.

Oh, here's some good dirt: I heard, from a reputable authority, that

Pavarotti couldn't read music—he got along using his phenomenal memory, and blew away the competition with his enormous voice and affable manner.

On the other hand, a stunning, slim woman in her prime, with the voice of an angel, was banned from the Met forever a few years ago, even though her appearances always meant sell-out crowds. The management must have been backed into a corner to resort to such a draconian decision, but she'd become impossible to work with. In my opinion, gorgeous coloratura soprano Kathleen Battle is the finest opera singer in the world. Her banishment was a tragedy.

Oops, I'm wandering...back to the point.

Once I was singing in the chorus of the opera *Carmen* in the Hill Auditorium at the University of Michigan, Ann Arbor. One cast member's toupee was dislodged, and inadvertently kicked around as characters shuffled about the stage, singing. Finally someone snatched it up—but it was too late; hilarity reigned in audience and chorus alike. Cries of "Olé" rang out amid scattered applause. Somehow, the cast managed to carry on, but the orchestra (blissfully unaware, their backs turned) and singers weren't in sync for a good while.

In high school, I attended an opera where the up-and-coming lead soprano experienced a complete lyric block. She couldn't remember her aria. Even intense prompting couldn't save her. Later it was revealed that she'd had one too many drinks, for courage.

To be fair, these sorts of incidents are infrequent. However, when multiple personalities, stagehands, puffed-up stars, animals, big orchestras and special effects are tossed together amid the glorious music, you might spot Chaos nestling quietly under the stairs, contemplating more than its navel...

My Iron Cinderella — Beauty in Chains

A CRISP AUTUMN DAY FIFTEEN years ago found me downstate at a farm auction sale that sounded interesting. (I'm a notorious scrounger.)

What an extraordinary place it was! The entire house leaned evenly, as though all the support beams had given up on the same day. Sun and wind had scoured off every scrap of exterior paint eons ago, but I thought the building retained a certain dignified, stark beauty.

Miscellaneous items filled the parched and weedy farmyard, which gave way to a dusty field. After a quick but thorough inspection I realized it was all junk; I'd driven all that way for nothing. Reluctant to face the long drive home just yet, I decided to explore the rest of the property.

I peered through the dirty windows of two decrepit outbuildings; both were empty. Despondent, I wandered toward the woods, and stiffened! A jumble of disjointed, linear ironwork, enveloped in weeds, was chained to the trunk of a bewhiskered, ancient oak tree. On my knees, parting the thicket, I exposed tangled cast-iron fence sections sandwiching three battered gates. They'd been abandoned here for far longer than I'd lived. Rust was dining on the thick chain and much of its intricate design; nevertheless, I felt a thrill! Here was a mid-nineteenth century work of art, forgotten and certainly doomed. Hopelessly in love, nervously fingering my cash, I tried to smother that smitten look: be charming, I muttered to myself—not eager.

Worried that some curious soul might wander near and discover my treasure, I loitered in the field at a safe distance the whole afternoon, pretending to be attached to the farm, watching its dissolution.

Finally, the last scavenger departed. While two strong men tossed unsold leftovers into the back of an old truck bed, I approached the grizzled, suspendered fellow who looked to be in charge. He was surprised to learn of the fence, and I kept my voice carefully casual as I asked if he'd sell.

Rubbing his hairy chin, he looked it over, then went to fetch a bolt cutter, as I itched to see the whole thing properly. We laid the fence sections on the ground; they measured 75.5 feet. I said something about confining my old dog, cheap, and he nodded, snapping his fat suspenders, but there was a gleam in his eye that told me this man wasn't born yesterday. After some haggling we agreed on a modest price, then loaded each rusting, flaking piece into my long-suffering old van.

I trundled off, my grin threatening to displace my ears. Later, skilled craftsmen sandblasted every inch, re-attached the broken bits, then powder-painted it forest green. The rest is history.

Research revealed that this graceful fence is at least 130 years old. Victorian artisans had formed delicate fans (instead of the more usual sharp points) at the top of each rod, and fashioned G clefs for its interior decoration, which delighted me as a musician. The ornate, matching gates now announce the garden's entrances and exits. Five leftover fan pieces decorate the huge hinges of my handmade wooden alley door, which itself included parts of the fence. Not a single scrap was discarded.

My rescued Cinderella frames our venerable Queen Anne Victorian home, displaying her delicate beauty and iron constitution to all who appreciate bygone craftsmanship. In winter, I savor each curve and intricate turn, beautifully showcased by the sculptured whimsies of wind-blown snow.

Spooky Machine Machinations

There are more things in heaven and earth, Horatio, than are dreamt of in your philosophy. —William Shakespeare, *Hamlet*

MYSTERIOUS MACHINATIONS HAPPEN whenever I approach certain machines. I must emit magnetic signals that encourage vacuums and toasters, for example, to vomit dust, flame out, or simply balk. The minute I sit down warily and eye my husband's laptop, the mouse freezes. The wretched machine won't even switch off!

But the most mystifying refusals happen with my two toilets.

To be blunt, these simple mechanisms dislike me. The drainpipes vibrate as they gurgle and mutter furtively, plotting watery ways to reject my offerings.

But why? I keep them clean. The Roto-Rooter man annually grinds away deep tree roots that grow into the sewer pipes, although only posh paper's dumped into their gaping mouths. I've done nothing to provoke them, ever.

My plumbing's ancient. Replacing the century-old, deeply buried tiles would mean massive excavations, thereby eliminating the garden. Unthinkable! So being solicitous makes sense.

The View From Sunnybank95

I've replaced most of the toilet's components. I've explored the downstairs loo with a flexible steel snake to induce decent swallows. Nada. So, reluctantly, the plumber was summoned. I flushed with a flourish to show how it would overflow; to my consternation, it worked perfectly! Arghhh!

Tutting and tsking, "monsewer" lectured at length on how to properly flush the loo (which took forever; the guy suffered from verbal diarrhea). Finally, he announced his diagnosis and treatment: raise the water level slightly, install a better lever, and adjust the tank chain to eliminate the problem. His storeroom housed the proper gadgets for the fix.

After three hours of seeking and tweaking, he pronounced it fixed. I was given a triumphant demonstration. Flushed with success, he proffered a bill for $240—house call fee, time, and labor—plus twenty-five dollars for parts. Mon Dieu!

The minute he left, it regurgitated. I refused to summon him again; a gold-plated gulper could be mine for that price. (But why bother? A new "privy's" plumbing would be no different.)

I've discovered how to beat the intermittent overflow problem: I hold down the lever until it swallows. This usually works. But when other people use it, what then? I've tried signs. They don't work.

A friend gifted me with an antique white porcelain urinal to cheer me up. I stuffed it with flowers and hung it up in the bathroom—but I'm still down in the dumps.

My late mother painted, framed, then posted me a lavishly decorated French Victorian toilet's portrait, complete with exposed plumbing and discreet wallpaper. These words appear:

C'est ici que tombent en ruines tous les talents de la cuisine.

Her artwork hangs cockily behind my miscreant, but the toilet is not amused.

In college I earned pocket money painting silly slogans on "throne" seats to sell to fraternities—stuff like:

The Pause That Refreshes
Feed Me
Watch For Alligators
Take It Or Leave It
Plop-Plop, Fizz-Fizz, Oh What A Relief It Is

Maybe my toilet's heard about these cheeky indiscretions; it's certainly old enough! (Gossipy exaggerations are probably exchanged through vast, interconnected sewer lines; these bored porcelain prima donnas thrive on all manner of dirt.) Maybe mine, having spookily dragged my collegiate past out of the water closet, now poops out its own version of Montezuma's Revenge. Maybe it's so politically sensitive that "toilet water" on my perfume bottle is enough to set it off. I dunno.

Meanwhile, the tank cover squats on the floor so I can monitor the evacuation situation. Perhaps today it'll relent, and accept deposits that won't return. Maybe, just maybe, it'll remember its mantra:

Abandon Hope, All Ye Who Enter Here

Machine Gripes — A Final Rant

"Pooh," you say, pondering last week's column. "Paranoid blather! Surely machines don't have it in for you!" Wanna bet?

Take my toasters. Their frequent flameouts flummox me. Once, I got lucky and chose one that was immune to my dubious magnetic charms; I mourned when it eventually died of old age. As for my current machine, I know its comfort zone; I just try to brown something bread-y without messing with the other options. Crumbs are regularly cleaned away. But still, it'll defiantly smoke, toast not at all, misread my settings, or perversely select its own.

"Well," you may mutter, "she probably buys cheap appliances." Nope. I've tried the posh route. Toast still burns, or is inadvertently abandoned because the "ping" indicating it's done fails to sound. My toast sits glumly in the dark, growing cold and stiff because I've forgotten to remember to retrieve it.

(Fascinating factoid: In England, unbuttered toast is routinely served cold. It's cut into tidy triangles and presented in silver racks, so air can properly circulate and stiffen each piece evenly. Scratch-scratch goes the butter knife, as exasperated Americans try to salvage the situation.)

Vacuum cleaners are another puzzlement. I've gone through every brand, cheap and steep: they all balk. I'm mystified. Mine is never forced to move over dangerous terrain. I ask only that it efficiently suck up hair, crumbs, dust bunnies, and the occasional dirt clot that might wander in from the garden. Nevertheless, it'll frequently refuse to eat; emit unbecoming, dusty belches; or simply stop. Suddenly, I'm powerless. But I don't panic. I'm not completely witless. Uh-huh, the plug's in, the bag's still willing, the brushes are unencumbered. (I heard that: you're thinking the wiring's insufficient, but mine is totally up-to-date.) I don't know what to do. Bribes don't work. It stays silent.

Other people's computers are jittery around me, but, happily, my new Macintosh has settled down, and (usually) accepts commands. I've learned to back up everything regularly, though, as whole columns can vanish when it gets addled.

Often, irrelevant information is tentatively proffered. Yesterday, it refused to bring up a letter I'd saved before answering the phone; instead, it crawled into the archives and trotted out an old recipe I'd forgotten about. I have no idea how, or why, that particular recipe was selected. Holding on to my temper, I quietly re-filed its offering, and coaxed the current letter to reappear. (Usually, if I stay calm, and don't lose it, or smack the keys, Mac complies, accepting that I'm dominant. But there's an undercurrent of provocation. The limits are regularly tested.)

The downstairs toilet continues to be intermittently fractious. Some days it behaves beautifully, and, foolishly, I'll begin to relax. But suddenly the tank won't fill; it'll run and run, until I catch it. These antics have cost us an appalling amount of wasted water. Posting a sign on the seat alerts other family or friends, but they'll often forget that final check when they leave the bathroom. You know the rest.

The garbage disposal couldn't care less. It dutifully devours any bone I throw it, then retreats into meditation. (Note: I inherited it.)

The thing is, recalcitrant machines teach patience. I count my blessings and look at the bright side. The loo could have decided to overflow, but, for its own reasons, this much less damaging irritation was selected instead. Like mosquito bites and thump-thump woofer noise, irascible toasters are part of my life; the sensible thing to do is to adapt without snarling.

My goal is always the same: don't kick 'em.

Little Disasters That Cheer Up God

I SOMETIMES FIND MYSELF TRYING to cope with spontaneous little disasters that happen when I'm distracted, unlucky, or way too full of myself.

At the farm auction where I acquired my antique iron fence, for example, I managed to perch atop a gentle mound that was actually a thriving anthill. The indignant creatures rushed out other exits because my bottom plugged their doorway. Quickly my sleeves, socks, and hair sprouted annoyed, bewildered ants, but fence-smitten, I didn't register what was happening until far too late.

For some reason the insects didn't bite, but their thousand tiny, tickling feet scurried in and out of every crease and crevice. Only when my hair felt alive, triggering brushing motions, did I grasp that I was raining ants.

I'd fervently wished to blend with the landscape; my fence-treasure had to remain undiscovered. "Be careful what you wish for," my mother used to say, her eyebrows wiggling like brown caterpillars.

I was one with the landscape that day. Fascinated people watched, slack-jawed, as I hopped around dislodging wee beasties; the auctioneer's garbled stream of words trailed off as my dance grew more vigorous. Eventually all the ants got the brush-off, I moved farther away, and nature and I settled down again, but the silly spectacle, where I felt smaller than my protagonists, created one of those comic scenes that cheer up God.

Years ago I met a dour potential garden client for tea. The restaurant was paved with thick grey carpet; muted classical music flowed from hidden speakers to lull diners into Zen-like states. With attentive waiters hovering, I pontificated about the pastry chef's homemade scones and crust-less sandwiches. This place represented my good judgment.

Unfortunately, a decent-sized cockroach jauntily jogged by my plate; against the cream tablecloth this perennial horror was impossible to miss. In a blink the atmosphere collapsed into ruins. Gesturing frantically to the waiter, I popped my empty tea cup over the beast, glumly acknowledging that, once again, the fickle finger of fate had found me fun to fiddle with. To add insult to injury, I still had to pay the tab. (Good judgment, eh? The lady, disillusioned and lacking a sense of humor, scurried away as soon as she decently could.)

In 1973, while backpacking in Italy, we stopped in Rome. Joe hadn't been abroad; I'd lived in Rome briefly. "I know," said I, with enormous confidence, "exactly where good, inexpensive lodgings are. We don't need the guide book."

As we exited the train an unkempt, ancient Roman with a practiced eye saw two suckers, so, making sleep-gestures, he indicated we should follow him to a hotel. This was too easy! A few turns later, we mounted rickety stairs to a gloomy room, with sheets that looked, well, suspicious. But pride goeth before a fall, so, instead of bailing, I paid.

After a miserable, car-honk, cat-yowly night we toured the usual places, but the heat was incredible, so we fled to Ireland—infested with lice. We writhed with lice. My favorite cap moved on its own; at the Dublin Horse Show, we couldn't sit still. Lice multiplied exponentially. Desperate, we begged a local pharmacist for help. He sold us three big bottles of lice-killer and directed our sorry selves to a nunnery. Stone-faced, those good ladies popped us into a huge, steaming, chemical-filled bathtub, tacitly condoning lice-death-by-dunking. Our clothes were taken away and fumigated. Submerged, eyes stinging, I sighed; once again, I'd defined "pompous idiot."

Now, a lifetime later, it's finally funny.

Mortal embarrassment has a long shelf life, God knows.

Knotty Thoughts: A Door Soliloquy

Gardening season better hurry up. —Dee's nervous husband

SOMETIMES, IN WINTER, WHEN I run low on music-making energy,
I think about doors. Door = snore. Most doors cause me to nod off,
as they are so uniformly unimaginative. They are carbon copies of
one another. Like mice. Most doors are rectangular. (Square doors
are rare doors.) They seldom inspire conversation. All doors have the
same hobby: they collect fingerprints, grease, and scuff marks.

Boring.

Even potato peelers have more fun.

Doors mostly hang around, waiting. They're very good at it. They aren't
loved. They aren't hated. They're ignored, and that's the worst curse.
They've developed no communication skills at all. (Well—maybe
they'll moan, or creak, or vibrate when slammed, or grumble when
"pocketed" in walls.) They display boring words that rarely exceed five
letters: Push, Pull, In, Out, Ladies, Gents. Most, though, are unnamed.

On the plus side, it isn't necessary to insure doors. They're seldom sick, and when they are, fixing what ails them costs two cents. (One squirt of WD-40, and they're cured.) Doors have stable personalities, rarely becoming unhinged. They are broad where a board should be broad, tolerate abuse, and are usually submissive and obedient, shutting people in/out, or welcoming even scruffy animals and humans without turning a hair—just their knobs.

Doors conform. They resist change. The five-panel look fits their nerdy comfort zone. Like classic clothes, this style is rarely out of style.

Infrequently, dysfunctional splinter groups, tired of being pushed around, break away to become tables, while retaining featureless plank looks and paper-thin veneers.

Many doors are flat as a prairie. (Modern ones are often hollow, gutless—all form, with no substance. Yet, these half-widths might become treasures; eager scientists in 3000 A.D. could test their entombed nine-hundred-year-old molecules to sample twenty-first-century air quality.)

Some doors get spiffed up, donning paint, stain, or sleek glassy looks; richer ones acquire big, impressive knockers, or artificially enlarged mouths that masticate mail, but, not being bright, doors never exploit these perks. They're content to hang on to brassy attachments and look good.

Sometimes ill-fitting doors host cotton snakes that cuddle up to, and along, their bottom lines, keeping drafts at bay. I have one of those. Snakes, that is (a.k.a. "draft-dodgers").

Sometimes doors are swingers, permanently non-committal. I had one of those, but chucked it. It would push back, smacking my nose, trying my patience.

Sometimes they'll boast a window. But you'll never find a windowed door to a bedroom, or bathroom. Ever. This is a Door Law.

Doors rarely die. (I've heard rumors of outdoor graveyards, but find the idea absurd. There's simply no proof.) They have a disconcerting tendency to live longer than we do. They just hang around, philosophical. Doors, if they had an opinion, would sum themselves up this way:

Whatever.

Perhaps this laissez-faire attitude explains why they live so long.

I doubt if doors retain even a tiny memory of what their lives as trees were like. Cellulose clogs (pervasive, but non-fatal) probably would block even simple dreams of, for example, "sawing logs" back and forth, back and forth...

Fascinating clues, like hardness, knots, and species, are ingrained, but doors are incurious. I do have proof that this is true; no one's ever heard doors express a longing for reverse reincarnation.

These sorts of deep, intense thoughts haunt me while I wait for gardening season to begin. I'll think about doors.

But just wooden ones.

Only sometimes.

(Other times, I might wonder what my DNA bits might wonder about, floating down the shower drain to...)

All Things Wise and Wonderful

ANIMALS DEMONSTRATE UNCANNY ABILITIES that we humans observe with wonder, but little understanding. The following is a true story.

A beloved relative of mine lives life with zest. She's a vivacious, multi-talented, intelligent woman who designed her own home, loves books, has a green thumb, and travels the globe, relishing her retirement.

Clare has always shared her home with cats; for many years three have claimed her as their own. (Any cat lover knows that felines decide who is important to them. Fiercely independent, they never fawn. They understand, more than we might like to admit, those humans they live with.)

Two years ago Clare was struck down by an autoimmune hepatitis that attacked her liver. This life-threatening illness severely weakened her. Trying to manage routine tasks—laundry, cooking, cleaning—exhausted her. Severe jaundice developed. After she endured extensive tests, a regimen of powerful medications was prescribed; her doctors told her time and rest would tell the tale. She thankfully took to her bed and slept away the weeks, awaiting events.

People she cherished helped, but her three cats, Tigger, Chloe, and Ladybug, went much further.

As a unit they moved into her bedroom and positioned themselves. One snuggled around her neck, one nestled in the crook of her arm or slept on her tummy, and one made sure her feet stayed warm. For many weeks they never left her, except to take turns grabbing a quick bite, and doing their toilets. They purred, massaged her with soft paws, and washed her with their rough tongues. Those cats were shadows, following her even to the bathroom. She was never alone. Her faithful felines monitored every breath. They were intertwined with the bedclothes, and such a part of her and each other it was hard to tell whose paws and tail belonged to whom.

One bright morning, she came awake slowly, aware of a distinct change in her environment; there were no sounds of purring. An unfamiliar lightness on her neck and chest jerked her to full consciousness; where for weeks there had always been cats—now there were none. By some mysterious means, the prescient trio knew she had passed a critical point, and would recover.

Amazed, Clare lay there, savoring the morning; a feeling of deep comfort and awe washed over her. She knew what their absence meant. In a week she would undergo more tests; they would show great improvement. Of that fact, she had no doubt. Her beloved friends had made the determination long before the doctors would.

She was right.

From that moment, Clare began to pick up the pieces of her life. The doctors, encouraged by her slow, steady progress, gradually tapered the potent medicines.

Further biopsies showed she just might recover without permanent liver damage. It was a near thing, though. She tired easily, and retreated to her bed for frequent naps. The furry trio, except for occasional quick, unobtrusive visits, let her sleep undraped.

It was an astounding demonstration of love, devotion, and their deep knowledge of the battle raging inside Clare. When they realized she would recover, perhaps through some chemical emitted that they recognized—(she'd finally "sniffed right")—they relaxed into their old routines without fuss.

Clare continues to rely on Tigger, Chloe and Ladybug to be astute monitors of her health.

She doesn't worry, if they don't.

Armchair Adventures and Spring Ghosts

GAZING OUT AT THE SNOWY garden, I fidget. After reveling in deep winter, I'm longing for workable, sun-warmed earth...Maybe I'll go out there with a hair dryer and hurry things along.

Today, though, I'm determined to thwart my packrat tendencies. Junk is proliferating in our attic. Thus, an industrial-strength garbage bag and I have marched up here; we won't leave until it's filled.

Whenever I trundle up these stairs and stir up the dust, it dances in the light. From here, the garden is a world away. There are no scents from it up here in the treetops. But the attic stinks of atmosphere. Unlike the rest of my house, this shuttered place has a peculiar privacy about it; it has a way of drawing my mind away from the task at hand.

The garbage bag rustles in my fist. I ignore the dust motes and look at where they're landing: on the suitcases. These are breeding rapidly. They've doubled in quantity over the years, and their little ones—travel-worn backpacks, knapsacks, carry-ons—are crowding me out. Ridiculous! Pretty soon we'll have to consider moving; these "et ceteras" are taking over the roomy, memory-filled, dusty, cluttered, junky space.

Look at that pile of books! Most of them I'm gonna vanish. But here's one I'll never part with: Spilling the Beans, the witty, eye-popping autobiography of seventy-year-old Clarissa Dickson Wright. What's it doing up here?! When I first brought this book home, I couldn't put it down. This brilliant, motorcycle-riding judge-turned-chef gave me quite a ride. She's unusually blunt, and full of outrageous, self-deprecating humor as well as deep insights. And she was fey, seeing ghosts as a young woman. My garbage bag sagged, the sun marched across the attic floor, time stopped.

Whoops! Ten-thirty. I'm gathering dust. The bag's still flaccid. I'm freezing, but in no time I warm up from dragging clothing-crammed boxes into the light, and shifting ancient furniture, including one giant old steamer trunk kids could practically camp in.

Nicer things will go to Goodwill, or be sold; the rest are gleefully chucked. Elderly boxes harbor defunct tree lights, broken Christmas bulbs, and frizzled styrofoam Santas. Tired piles of old paperbacks, and stiff, dead shoes are scattered around, cuddled by fat dust bunnies—what was I thinking?!

Awk! Here's another gem! M.C. Beaton's delightful Hamish Macbeth mystery peered up at me from the rubble. I snatched it up happily, remembering the fun of reading about this complicated red-haired policeman's latest professional adventures. Hamish's rapport with his dog and cat and his run-ins with the obnoxious Chief Inspector Blair make for lively reading. Wow! Scottish village life is never dull.

Focus, Dee. Blinking, I dismiss Scotland. Bins of clothes await me. Most of these are strictly for the mice. But, Oh! Our children's infant outfits are hugged close. These are treasures. Only yesterday Jen and

Lisa trotted off to kindergarten with Kermit beaming on this jumper, and the Cookie Monster looking hopeful on that lunch box. I gaze outside my aerie's grubby window and sigh, hearing my daughters singing Sesame songs.

Enough! That bag's only half-full. As I stagger to my feet, my knees pop.

Suddenly, I spot something. Over in a dark corner, about waist-high, where the roof rafters move toward the floor, a curved, metallic, and vaguely familiar object was wedged between huge, time-darkened rafters. It resists my probing fingers, but I pull and tug. Finally, out pops an ancient rug beater! Looking it over, I distinctly hear a small boy's triumphant whisper: "She'll never find it here!" The roots of my hair tingle. I look around.

It's not the first time this house has hinted at lives that thrived here a century ago. Many poignant memories have permeated these stout timbers, to echo gently in receptive ears. Perhaps my parental, olden-days sigh has prompted the house to give up this one.

I shiver, smile, and say, softly, "No, she never did…"

Wishy-Washy brooms vs. Brooms

AS BIRTHDAYS COME FASTER, I often contemplate how in life there are three constants: death, taxes, and bad brooms.

To wit, there are brooms, and Brooms. Similarly, there are people who sweep, and then there are Sweepers. Usually, brooms are wielded by sweepers in a desultory manner; trash feels unthreatened; crisp, finished edges are unknown. The sweeper is NOT master of the situation. Even when wielding a proper Broom, perfectly designed to whisk away objectionable debris, many sweepers haven't a clue. They shweep.

Teamwork is essential.

Sweeping properly is extremely important. If I interviewed an apprentice, the first thing I'd do is put a Broom in her hand, and ask her to have a go. I'd immediately grasp what sort of worker she'd be. Would she Sweep with authority? Would she maneuver the Broom, cleverly clearing cracks? Would she use broad Sweeps, and not crab along with useless, no-pressure little-old-lady motions? I demand a Commander! What I usually get are shweepers—broom wimps.

Let's examine the tool itself.

A common kitchen broom sports slick nylon bristles which bend easily and are clipped at a rakish angle, reminiscent of a skinny model wearing a shimmery Sassoon haircut. The slim, bright blue, green or even crackerjack-red plastic handle is screwed or glued into its holding hole, which goes wobbly after just a few jobs. The annoyed operator winds up re-securing it, over and over. Sigh... Trash, distinctly unfrightened, yawns.

Other brooms look traditional. These might have the classic long wooden handle that fits nicely into a receptacle at the top of the business end; the straw is cut straight, and feels okay. But the handle has a subtle but telltale spareness, and the bristles—like thinning hair expertly blown dry to appear thicker—are insubstantial. They'll go limp when asked to perform.

Alas, a test run is never done. People see a reasonable-looking broom, and, lured by the red stitching and traditional look, they snatch it up and trot to the checkout counter. Only later do they realize they've bought a broom. Their hands know something isn't right; the thing feels oddly inadequate somehow. Hushing their inner voice, they'll shweep dutifully, secretly puzzled by the lackluster results. Snicker-snack, their tool will develop broom-bottom-sag, which is incurable. The baffled shweeper shrugs.

I own Brooms. Each is well-made. Hefty. The long handle is thicker than its doppelganger; it's made of hardwood. No cute color has been applied. A stout screw insures there'll never be bristle-wibble.

The business end is heavy. If a fascinated buyer holds this Broom up against the other one, the difference is instantly obvious. It's got muscle. THIS plain stitching is like iron. There are many more densely compacted bristles, which are cut thick, straight and even, with a wide, stiff skirt. Those stout ends resist sag. This. Broom. Sweeps. It's a work of art, honed after centuries of tweaking.

Of course, because these Brooms are constantly used, their bristles will shorten, shortly. Wise operators retire exhausted Brooms, then march out to farm or hardware stores for another, which, of course, they'll wisely test. Experienced Sweepers keep bristles protected when the tool is resting. Some even store Brooms upside-down, to prevent their bristles from snagging.

I've worn out many a stalwart Broom. Trash trembles; edges gleam. Together, we make clean sweeps!

Talkin' Trash: A Scavenger's Tale

When visiting my daughters in Chicago, I haunt architectural salvage centers, where all manner of intriguing stuff is recycled from buildings targeted for demolition. Salvage One, a favorite, offers iron fences similar to my trashed treasure, as well as intriguing tubs, toilets (crammed with gleaming porcelain flowers), leggy sinks, beautifully carved fireplace mantels, zillions of decrepit, delightful doors, banisters, wall paneling rescued from decaying mansions—and sometimes, If I'm lucky, chipped treasures pried from abandoned gardens. I blew the dust off a smallish, battered old faun face buried under a pile of copper pipes. The dinged ear and age-blurred features didn't detract from this rogue's sly grin, which suggested a tawdry mystery-history. I had to have him.

Half the fun is dickering. Worn jeans, dusty jackets, rumpled hair and dirty hands keep the price down.

Today it's much harder to scavenge overlooked treasures; sellers know better. Rummage sales, however, sometimes yield up gems. Sorting through stuff that languished on the porch of one home, years ago, I spotted a heavy, museum-quality rectangular planter huddled in the corner, housing a heap of old, dead boots. Living there so long, it had become invisible. The startled owner happily palmed thirty dollars. Grinning, I staggered off with my weighty treasure, which writhed with chipped, classical figures that still wear a hint of moss-green paint. Bright red geraniums look delightful in its generous planter.

It's fun to think out of the box. Once, years ago, I pounced on an ancient pump organ; rats had dined on its leather bellows. Fortunately the black walnut case, sporting delightful 1880s woody ruffles and flourishes, was ignored by the other treasure-hunters. The entire front half (with its rotting, toothy keys extracted) became our library mantel, complete with music stand. The lovely side panels wandered below stairs into our homemade wine cellar to transform a dented, metal lazy Susan cupboard that had once lived to twirl in the kitchen. Wearing posh, chocolate-colored walnut sides now, it happily houses wine glasses.

Other organ donations appear here and there around the house. Nothing was wasted.

Lacy or floral cotton-blend on-sale shower curtains make attractive, durable outdoor tablecloths. They aren't afraid of soap and water, and don't wrinkle, or faint from repeated washings. (Anyone who sniffs at the holes-for-hanging needs to get a life.) Sometimes I must detach extra panels of ruffles on top. Even tables have limits; they flatly refuse to accommodate this extra baggage.

Most of my fountains were once elderly, discarded pillars or birdbaths. Our careful restoration did wonders, and now their water music plays amid tranquil garden scenery.

Thin, flexible cedar house siding, sixteen feet long, lines the garden borders along my winding paths. I've sunk the first two inches into the earth, exposing the rest to weather. We curved the ends, which makes them friendlier to ankles. Replacement every few years is cheap and easy.

Errant hoses ruin flowerbeds. Inexpensive antique colored glass insulators, with foot-long sharpened dowels poked into their fat heads, then "grounded," transform these objects into interesting hose guides. I think they look nicer than the vivid green plastic whachamacallits sold everywhere. Or I might insert brass doorknobs, with stems still attached, into slim black buried PVC pipe. Hoses are discreetly, imaginatively managed; flowers feel safer.

Picking through a Welsh garden center's rubbish tip eleven years ago I found a lovely, beautifully detailed cement eagle with a broken wing. Mended now, it decorates a fence pillar. I love that bird.

Battered "sows' ears" can become treasures you'll use, unlike those "boaring" (and useless) silk purses. Thinking out of the box requires slightly skewed vision and imagination, but the results are rewarding!

Ducks Consider Gardener a Quack

WELL. JOE AND I SPENT April in England visiting family, enjoying the lush spring, and renewing friendships. Home again, we've discovered that a pair of mallards has moved into the main garden. They swim happily in my big, rain-filled fountain pool, pooping regularly to season it. Ugh.

Romeo's pleased with his Juliet, and she with him; they're rarely more than a foot apart. They wander happily through the rapidly growing beds, nibbling greenery, snapping up foolish slugs and bugs, and planning a family. I keep peeking under the big Chamecyparis, praying she hasn't laid eggs under its thick shelter. Mallard families can be large—imagine ten babies zipping around! Surely these ducks aren't that dim; Cat would dispatch eggs and infants quicker than instantly.

The lovebirds are getting far too comfortable. They quack endearments; the male lays his shining head on her back, and the two stand quietly in the sun, enjoying each other's company.

He has a favorite bed, smack in the middle of the lush patch of woolly thyme next to the pool. Ducks have a poor reputation for minding their manners when faced with its soft charms. So far, though, Romeo has refrained from ruining it.

Nevertheless, yesterday I marched right up to him, reduced myself to his level and announced that I would not tolerate any vandalism; if he pecked just once at my thyme, both were dinner.

There we were, beak to nose, inches apart. He heard me out, quacked quietly, rearranged his feathers, and simply went to sleep.

You'd think he'd be intimidated! I threatened to wring his gorgeous neck, pop him into a hot oven and roast him for dinner! I hollered that proper ducks should be down by the river. I warned him that drinking that, er, "rich" water would make him sick, impotent, or worse. Nada. My warnings about fowl play were clearly water off his back. Disgusted, all I could do was to stalk off, muttering bird-brained insults.

I wish they'd get gone! I have work to do. I should drain and scrub the pool. (But if I do, they'll fowl it!) I must chainsaw the huge miscanthus grasses, redo the drip irrigation, transplant and clean the winter-worn beds. But I'm constantly tripping over lovesick ducks.

Jet lag wears me out. I need five days to readjust to Michigan time; meanwhile, I feel like dog food. Clearly, these orange-footed featherheads won't budge. There's nothing I can do without courting a headache.

Yesterday I wearily plopped down on the big bench for a brief rest—and woke up thirty minutes later with a start. R and J were beaking my cargo pants, trying to dislodge a button. No sense sharpening my fangs. They know I don't have any.

Where is that darn cat? One glimpse of him would surely send them flapping. But he seems to have vanished.

After naps Juliet sometimes follows me around, watching me work. She'll offer an occasional nasal comment or suggestion, which I studiously ignore.

But mostly, they have eyes only for each other. She eggs him on all the time; it's hard to concentrate with all that lovemaking going on. Feathers are rumpled, orange feet flap, and ecstatic quacks ring through this proper Victorian garden. Humph...

Nothing ruffles their feathers afterward. The chainsaw's roar is ignored, noisy workmen tweaking my giant tulip tree put them to sleep, and all my vigorous digging and wheelbarrowing only makes them yawn. Passion wears them out.

But that's love. I'm just background noise. It's disconcerting to be so thoroughly dismissed.

Good thing I have a strong ego.

Falling in Love with Trashed Toenails

I KNOW, I KNOW...WHADDAYA do with someone who thinks like this? I dunno, but my husband has adapted, so I guess there's hope that I'm salvageable.

Truth is, I love toenails, especially the ones I discovered in a battered rubbish bin behind an antique shop. Let me explain.

Four seasons ago we visited a posh store in Saline, Michigan, that featured gorgeous imported French and English antique furniture. Its generous outdoor garden area, though, really grabbed my attention. Arches, iron fences, pools, statuary, hand-carved benches, and lots of Victorian urns waited hopefully for an appreciative buyer. But my hands stayed relaxed, my eyes looked around without widening, and my breathing remained regular—until I snooped around the back. In a lean-to shed a pile of crumbling pillars sagged against the corrugated wall, propped up by one broken lead planter, a Victorian chimney pot whose top had disappeared, and a bench long past its sell-by date.

It was then that I struck gold! In their huge trash can, stuffed with dead urns, fence rods, and splintered wood, some magnificent white toenails, on what looked suspiciously like griffins' feet, poked forlornly out of the rubble, revealing just enough to set my heart racing. Wow! Those ruined talons hooked me.

Carefully I began extracting all the chunks. Finally, seven pieces, which included the flat tops that a bench seat would normally rest on, lay scattered on the dirt. Kneeling, I tried to match talons with ankles, ankles with legs, till I had both sets more or less connected. Whew! It would take time and ingenuity to make them look sharp again.

A final rummage deep into the interior to retrieve smaller pieces and slivers, a quick dust-off, and then I trotted off to find the guy in charge. He smoothed his chin, and sighed. "Lady, these bench legs are goners. If you want 'em, they're yours." He looked sideways at Joe, pity in his eyes.

Oh boy! I had to firmly squash my joy; a triumphal whoop might make him rethink the gift. Gently I loaded each heavy piece into the van, while my husband rolled his eyes. As we drove home I extolled their virtues for at least a hundred miles, full of confidence in my ability to put Humpty back together again.

It's funny; I go all fuzzy with delight when I see or feel soft, dangly tassels, or fringe attached to anything. Similarly, those toenails sent me into a bliss that's lasted for years. You must admit that romantic, gleaming white, toenailed griffin-legs are vanishingly rare. Like griffins.

Well, we mended them, using a special, pale glue that blended well. They look wonderful in the Brick Walled Garden by the Victorian fountain. With a proper bench seat to top it off, the effect is smashing.

I got the same rush when I rescued the semi-ruined Ram's Head Fountain. Breathing was difficult, my hands clenched, my eyes popped. It, too, boasts absurd and wonderful ram-feet. Les's clever fingers re-created missing bits with cement filler. Look closely and you'll see the color differences that betray his work. But who cares? Quirky is good.

Some people like bosoms. Some admire behinds. For me, though, taloned toes on mythical legs equal rapture.

Nanny Trees Stump Bully, Lend Support

I'VE ALWAYS BEEN AN ARBOREAL creature. I cherish my garden's trees; each has a distinct personality, or a particular shape or talent. The tulip tree showers brides with its petals in early June. My hazel tree showed elegantly against a snowy backdrop. Reincarnated tree parts form my fence, as well as my ornate posts, flowerbed containment boards, and benches. Strong, wide, hand-cut boards lavishly decorate Sunnybank House. Heavy, handmade, arched wooden doors introduce my secret garden retreat. Wooden handles anchor my tools; wooden spoons stir my porridge; and trees are transformed into my favorite well-thumbed books.

When I was little, my mother was forever finding me under, or in, a big chestnut tree in our yard. Elegant and mature, my nanny tree had miraculously escaped the builders' flatten-the-earth rush to erect post-war housing. I loved playing with my wooden pull-toy dog, Snuffy-Sniff, under her huge branches. I'd climb up into those inviting arms, using my tricycle seat as a stepladder to grasp the first accommodating limb. There I'd be, dangling happily, my bright red overalls making me easy to spot.

Trees are essential, still, to me. I love how they arch high above my street, beautiful in all seasons. Their lush, sheltering, leaf-laden branches offer cool refuge in summer; thigh-thick, gnarled roots spill from their bases to amuse themselves (and annoy local officials) by heaving up Traverse City's sidewalks.

Intriguing holes, high up ample trunks, are homes to birds, who vanish into them with worm-crammed beaks. If I'm lucky I'll see babies poke their heads outside each spring, gasping at the vast world far below.

Big, strong trees command respect. Roped planks attest to their willingness to accommodate swings for youngsters over the centuries. Even today, a nanny tree tempts me to sway and dream, or climb as high as I dare. I find them irresistible.

When I was about ten I was constantly persecuted by Douglas, a spider-limbed bully who was determined to rip at my thick braids, and to kick my schoolbooks into dusty Sutton Street, simply because he could. I'd never exchanged a single word with him, but he taunted me tirelessly. I soon learned to keep my face inert, and he got even angrier when I wouldn't react.

One day, the nuns rulered his hands. One piercing, white-hot glance from him in the drinking fountain line told me where he'd vent his rage. I knew, with a child's instinct for these things, that that day he would try to really hurt me. He was dangerous. When we were released from school I ran down the dusty road to my oak tree as if the very devil were after me. Like a squirrel I climbed it from the back, out of view, higher and higher, panting with the effort. He thundered down the lane moments later, hot with frustrated rage and pain, screaming my name. But I had vanished. Baffled, he kicked the trunk, hurled stones, and spit incoherent threats. It never occurred to him to look up. If he had, it wouldn't have mattered. I clung to that solid bulk, enveloped in an ocean of leaves, my green plaid uniform skirt blending perfectly with her lush foliage. That oak nannyed me when I needed it most. (Soon after, his family moved: my world felt fresh and new.)

Today, from my own bedroom window, I watched a black squirrel peep out of his roomy hole-home in the big maple along the wet street. Together, high and dry, we quietly enjoyed the spring rain, sheltered and safe in our snug, woody havens, grateful that nanny trees, in whatever form they assume, lend solid reassurance and constancy to Mother Earth's children.

Bowser's Beastly Adventure

THE OTHER DAY I WAS conversing with a neighbor who'd stopped to chat after seeing me in the alley, watering. Eventually she tied her attractive little grey dog, Bowser, to one of my enormous, empty plastic rubbish bins by the garage. He accepted this philosophically. Then she and I went into the garden to retrieve some plants she'd agreed to adopt. They'd been divided and cleaned, and needed a home. Joanie's lovely garden was perfect.

Suddenly, a tremendous clatter shattered the peaceful morning. From deep within the garden we glimpsed the giant bin thundering past the half-open alley gate, with an attached grey blur leading the way.

We knew instantly what was unfolding. Bowser had spotted ancient Cat oh-so-slowly doing his daily rounds, and, naturally, he did what any respectable canine would do. Forgetting he was firmly tied to the bin, he'd launched himself down the broad asphalt lane toward his prey.

Then, out of nowhere, a cavern-mouthed Thing began hotly pursuing HIM!

Such a roar! Such mega-yowls! Such horrific howls from protesting plastic! The bin lid flew off, becoming an unguided missile that attacked a telephone pole along the rough road. Out of the corner of his eye, Bowser noted the hit without processing it, while he prayed for wings; naturally, his long leash refused to loosen from the Thing's lip, to give a dog a break. Bowser couldn't spare the breath to bark; instead, he tried weaving, in a desperate effort to escape—but the empty-bellied Thing, huge mouth agape, seemed determined to crunch him. He'd be cat food!

Cat, riveted, watched thankfully from the sidelines. This was much more interesting than his usual naptime "Mighty Cat" fantasies about stalking, then pouncing on, sleeping dogs and inattentive mice, by golly. Moreover, this was Justice, long overdue.

By the time we reached the alley gate the shocking bin-roars had stopped; quiet reigned. Bowser had vanished. Joanie began calling him. We peered around garage corners and looked under bushes—nothing. Eventually, a good distance away, she located the bin, lying on its side near a parked car by somebody's back yard. Bowser, still connected to it, had found sanctuary under the car. There was no panting, no response to Joanie; he was a saucer-eyed statue.

Joanie tugged gently and continued to call his name as she disconnected the leash from the offending bin. Finally, she coaxed him out. He stood quietly, deep in thought, gazing into space…What had just happened? Was this payback for all those years of thrilling cat-pursuits? Maybe moth-eaten mousers had one wish each. Maybe that cat had used it.

Bowser absolutely knew he was meant to love his family, enjoy regular meals, poo, sniff the news, and chase squirrels and cats. Life made sense. He knew what was what.

Yet…had he got it wrong? In an instant, everything he'd assumed about how things worked had been turned upside down. It was a puzzling old world.

Joanie collected her plants, and she and Bowser made their way home. His legs automatically walked, but Bowser's mind was clearly elsewhere.

Cat, sitting quietly near our gate, washed his paws, thoughtfully. He, too, was processing his wonderful deliverance. Perhaps, just perhaps, old cats could deter death-by-dog by simply wishing fervently for Mighty Cat payback, as he'd done when Bowser had begun his rush to judgment. Too old to run, Cat knew he was dog food—until The Miracle happened.

It was a fascinating old world...

Alley Adventure Still Haunts Bowser

I MET JOANIE AND BOWSER yesterday in the alley. She told me he'd shot her a look of incredulity when she'd guided him toward the alley, where his beastly adventure of a week ago had occurred. Clearly, he was still mulling over that event. Extremely wary, he walked the route with stiff legs and swiveling neck. Nervous vigilance ruled. It didn't take a rocket scientist to guess that Bowser was dreading the appearance of Cat and Cat's terrifying trash-can minion. Here was a splendid example of one-trial learning.

I suspect his angst was alley-specific. Bowser would probably fling himself into a vigorous chase anywhere else, but here he felt a worrisome "ping" in the back of his mind. Might the mouth-monster decide to appear wherever he went?

Still...

Alley pooing was out of the question; constipation had become a problem, of late.

"He is a bit better every day. Time will tell," commented an amused Joanie.

Bowser, trying to master invisibility, tiptoed by.

"Flowered" Elk Lake Memories

ONCE UPON A TIME, long ago, I spent my summers at Elk Lake, near Traverse City. A vast forest surrounded our large cabin, high on a lake-view hill. There were no people for miles, so I amused myself observing forest life. At ten, I moved quietly through that green world, marveling.

Chipmunks caught my eye. They were so cheerful! So irrepressible! Zip! Zoop! They'd whiz busily here and there, cheeks fat with collected edible bits and pieces gathered while attending spontaneous chipmunk conventions in the meadow. I could hand-feed one bold fellow, after some coaxing; the others shouted that he was an idiot, from a safe distance. "Chippie" was today's equivalent of a rebellious teen...

With a gleam in his eye he'd boldly accept some toast, then dart off, triumphant.

I can still summon intrigued chipmunks with the chippy-chirp call I learned there. It's one of my more interesting talents. (Veterinarian-author James Herriot boasted that he could expertly wrap a cat, exposing only the relevant part for safe examination. We humans tend to treasure our tiny triumphs.)

I learned to love morning smells. Mother's slim fingers would surround a mug of pungent coffee; she'd stand quietly at the window, listening to Rachmaninoff, thinking thoughts she never shared.

I'd often make the mile-long round trip to the mailbox with her. We glimpsed deer only occasionally, though they had been watching us much longer. Yearlings would eye us curiously as we navigated the narrow, rutted dirt road that wound through the thickly wooded forest.

One day I literally stumbled upon a fawn, lying absolutely still in golden dappled forest sunlight. Though I'd nearly stepped on him, not an eyelash moved. I gave a yelp, and froze, wailing, "He's dead!" But she said, softly, "Not dead. He's hiding in plain sight. Back away; don't touch. His mother's desperate for us to go." Just five feet away the sun-speckled baby "disappeared" into the foliage; it was my first experience with practical magic.

I often played under the house foundations. One morning, as Beethoven thumped above me while my mother cleaned, I heard rustling noises; simultaneously, an indescribable smell assaulted my young nose. A gorgeous, perfectly groomed skunk padded serenely past, unafraid. Though horrified, I had the sense to remain absolutely still. Two feet away she paused to examine me. We exchanged long, thoughtful looks, while she made up her mind about whether I needed a bath. I forgot to breathe. Please, no, I thought. No…

Her perfume was awful. I knew I'd probably spend the next week on a moss bed well away from the cabin if she spritzed me. But that morning she didn't feel like sharing. An eternity passed. At last, Madame resumed her walk, not once looking back, satisfied that she was respected.

Recalling Disney's skunk, "Flower," made me laugh; then, retching, I ran down to the lake and jumped in, relieved beyond measure.

Elk Lake stocked its own fascinating wildlife. If I waded near the rocky shore, delighted leeches would rise from their submerged pebble beds, clamber onto my ankles and grow fat with my blood; I quickly learned to swim, just to avoid becoming a meal.

Nights were the best. The stars were bright jewels in a velvet-black setting; Sputnik moved silently among their twinkles. I dreamed of flying.

Occasionally, the Northern Lights would stun the imagination. I didn't know how to frame intelligent questions, but merely stared, gasped, and fell asleep, tumbling into shifting, water-colored dreams.

A Pork-Pie Hat's Blustery Adventure

IT'S A BLUSTERY DAY. THIS sort of weather always gets my heart beating too fast. I fret about my taller, slimmer plants, and begin to run around flapping my hands, rather like a chicken with the usual problem. One of my worries is the threat posed by the sixty-foot tall, ramrod-straight tulip tree that looms over everything. Heavy football-shaped seed casings drop from his tall, stately branches onto heads and beds in summer. Big winds could push him over or bring down more footballs. I stay well away from General Tulip before thunderstorms. I hope he stays away from my house.

In short, a windy day is an anxious time. Mostly I do a few essential steadying fixes, then practice Zen-like resignation as I retreat to the kitchen. But I chew my nails.

One exceptionally windy day, an ancient, wizened man, his body bent like a comma, wandered slowly through the main garden. Suddenly, a fierce gust snatched away his weathered pork-pie hat, whirled it around, then deposited it high up in the maple tree by the garage. I heard a shouted curse. In a twinkling the elderly gentleman had snatched a broom, grabbed a ladder I'd been using, and, propped it against the garage, then nimbly scrambled up its rungs to retrieve his treasure. He'd reached the ladder's top and was preparing to climb onto the roof next to the tree, broom in hand, when, amazed and concerned, I rushed there to steady it. Seeing me, he called down firmly, "I want my hat. I ain't leavin' without 'er."

I yelled up that I had a good idea, and would he please come down so I could demonstrate a safer way to get it back? He perched there uncertainly, looking doubtful, then sighed and confidently backed down, brushing aside my offer to help hold the ladder. I sagged with relief as he stood before me, expectantly.

Trotting to the garage I fetched a long, slim rope, tied a stone on one end, and tossed it up into the greenery as close to the hat as I could. But I missed. After three throws the gentleman lost patience, grabbed the line from me and threw it perfectly. One quick flick and down came the hat, none the worse for its adventure. He smacked it into shape and plunked it on his head, snorting with satisfaction. "My wife gave me this thing. She's gone now, but I wear it to remind myself of how she covered all my bases. She was a fine woman. Oh yeah, I was a sailor in the Second World War, so I got good balance, missy."

Holding it firmly in place he thanked me, said I needed throwing lessons, grinned, winked and departed.

I sat down, still unnerved. He could have fallen. He could have died!

Suddenly, I realized that I'd assumed he was frail because of his advanced age. His dead-on aim and nonchalance high up the ladder in strong winds showed that premise to be false. "Old" doesn't always mean decrepit.

Darn! I wish we'd talked. Imagine the stories stored under that hat!

Duckling Delights, Mama's Mistake

WHILE WASHING DISHES AND humming a tune, I heard a familiar but muted quack. From the kitchen window I saw Juliet Mallard strut confidently into the Fairy Garden, followed by five fluffy ducklings in a neat line behind her pert tail. (Visitors had inadvertently left the first gate open.) Padding over the lush Irish moss, she quack-commented on its softness, then waddled to the Fairy Fountain. The little ones bumped to a stop and crowded around the edge of the four-foot-wide pool, thrilled by the water tumbling from the big fairy statue. She quacked permission-to-swim, and the infants excitedly plopped into the water, peeping and paddling around the small circle while Mama watched indulgently from the sidelines. After a bit she assumed a more comfortable position and preened her feathers, listening to their delighted cheeps with amusement. Clearly, she'd planned this outing.

Wait a minute—where was Romeo? He was usually close by. I ran to the living room window. Aha! He'd settled down on the sun-warmed front lawn, tucked bill into feathered back, and fallen asleep. I rushed back to the kitchen window; the kids were splashing about happily, reminding me of excited children discovering Disneyworld's water rides. High-pitched mini-quacks told me they'd "ducked" under the gentle waterfall. Soft breezes would occasionally ruffle drooping ferns, which tickled their tiny heads. Initially alarmed, they'd heard no "take cover" signs from Mama, so their tiny bodies relaxed into the experience.

It was fascinating that she knew not to join them. It would have been too crowded. No, let the kids have their fun; it was quite safe in that snug, sheltered corner of the garden.

Eventually though, there were signs of restlessness. Juliet was looking bored. Curious, I decided to go out there, just to see what might happen.

I passed the sleeping Romeo; useless as a guard, he never noticed. But as soon as I entered the Fairy Garden and approached, Madame silently faced me; opening her beak wide she stood tall and spread her wings, shielding her children, reminding me to keep my distance.

Testing, I took a step toward her. One firm quack and the kids vacated the water. She efficiently herded them under the giant, plumed *Aruncus* right next to the fountain, quacked another stay-away command, then joined them underneath its ground-skimming branches. She knew me and wasn't alarmed, but the rules were clear: I was not to approach, period.

If I hadn't known better I wouldn't have guessed that six souls were five feet away. They'd vanished. Not a peep came from the babies. No movement. I waited. Nothing. Romeo, her champion, snored on out front, oblivious.

Impressed, I stepped back, opened the big gate wider so her brood and she could leave, and retreated to the house. Back at the kitchen window I saw her quack "all's clear;" everyone tumbled out—then,

Shock, Horror! Mama pooped copiously on the delicate, blossoming Irish moss, then once more. That did it. The park was closed! I began to dog-pant and meow loudly from the window. Wary, she looked around, then stared right up at me. Oops! Nevertheless, I persisted, determined to eliminate the eliminator. (Moss cleanup is frustratingly difficult.)

Though she certainly knew who was behind these pathetic imitations, Juliet had had enough. A quick quack assembled the ducklings; they paraded out, up the pine-needled path, and onto the front lawn. Collecting Romeo, she waddled confidently to the curb, crossed over, and led everyone tidily to the river.

Sighing, I began mop-up operations.

Mushy, mossy mallard messes make me mutter. But it's the price of playing hostess.

All That Glitters: A Padlock's Tour

I'VE MANAGED TO SOLVE a vexing problem: the main fountain is free of avian deposits because I place a tarp over its bulk every evening. Then, after securing it, I insert small orange pole-mounted flags into the ground around the pool. Happily, their fluttering seems to deter birds. Now crows and ravens roost elsewhere, saving me a tedious cleanup every morning.

But yesterday a fascinated crow flew down to inspect one bright flag. He pecked at the plastic banner, trying to dislodge it. It proved a bit too pole-high to snatch, but his attempt to steal it made me thought-ful. Crows are wily birds; he could conceivably figure out how to yank the slim metal pole free, as only a tiny bit of it was shoved into the earth. I watched the creature sit, pondering, atop the fence, head cocked, trying to work it out. Orange is obviously a tremendous lure for birds with a flair for design.

Since observing this behavior, I count flags every morning. One never knows.

A tiny, shiny brass padlock that secures the Brick Walled Garden gate has proved similarly irresistible to young children. I went outside to lock up in the evening recently, only to discover it gone. (I'd seen a small boy fiddling with the chain there, but hadn't made the connection. I keep forgetting to close it during the day. Now, I was glad that the package had contained a spare.)

Yesterday two small children wandered hand-in-hand into the garden. The bigger boy, about seven, led a tiny girl, perhaps three, around the main fountain, pointing out its decorative swans, "flying" with his arms to demonstrate. Eventually they arrived in the Brick Walled Garden. Curious, I listened at the library window.

"Oh," she cried, spotting the new (whoops!—still unsecured) "gold" padlock. "a wock-it-up!" As she fiddled with it, it disconnected from the slim chain and landed in the palm of her hand.

Her smile was radiant. She clutched it tightly, reached for her brother's hand, and tugged it, suddenly eager to leave. But the boy had observed her furtive palming of this treasure, and firmly told her to put it back.

Instantly her face clouded. She gave forth an unequivocal "NO!" "You gotta," he insisted. "It isn't yours!" With impeccable logic, she declared, "It's MINE! It WIKES me. It CAME to me!" Tears began to form; her fingers tightened protectively. Clearly, she wouldn't give it up without a fight.

The boy, dismayed, thought hard. Then he looked her full in the face and said, "Lots of people like you. What if some lady you didn't know took you home with her? Would you like that?"

This was a troubling thought. The child's eyes grew huge. "No!" she declared, her lip trembling.

"Well," said the boy, more confidently, "that's how this wock-it-up feels. It lives here. Let's take it around the garden. It'll be all yours, just for the walk. Then you gotta put it back where it belongs."

She thought about this, then slowly nodded. He released a slow, relieved breath. Off they went, padlock-in-hand. The garden bell was duly rung again; they strolled among the flowers, discovering things they'd missed before.

Eventually, they returned to the final gate. She carefully hooked the wock-it-up into the tiny chain, and patted it sadly. But there was no more resistance.

As wise teacher and budding diplomat, this little boy was pure gold.

Eavesdropping On Teen Talk

UNDER A HUGE HOSTA, I pulled weeds, looked for slug-sign, and checked my giant ornamental onions for evidence of rambunctious baby onions. Growl...My stomach suddenly complained, and I felt hungry enough to consider emerging. Then the garden bell rang. Large sneakered feet padded by my dark haven. Hmmm... untied shoelaces, no socks, and tanned, hairy legs. A teenage boy. The shoes paused; the attached voice commented, "Radical...somebody gets off on spiders! Yo! Check out this black fountain."

Another voice, still inside the gatehouse, yelled, "Hey! A weird head's hangin' high in here... It looks like your retarded botany teacher on Monday mornings." (Loud chortles followed this pronouncement.)

Voice Two trotted into the garden toward his sneakered companion. They both stood awhile, looking, then wandered to the main bench and plopped down. Very long black T-shirts draped their tall, angular frames; their black shorts (more like abbreviated pants, but three sizes too large) were bedecked with zippers and gleaming, fob-like chains (which probably held wallets and keys) that disappeared into pockets. The tightly belted, crotch-at-knees garments clung precariously to narrow lower pelvises. The laws of gravity had been successfully defied.

Voice One began pointing to plants, launching into a commentary. "I know that big yellow triangle shrub. My granddad's got one, a cam-a-sip—whatever. He likes growing stuff that doesn't make work. And that's a flowering vine climbing up the spider web, named Clementine, or whatever—and those sword-blade ones in front of everything are iris. See? They come in two outfits. The green and white leaves look pretty decent all year. Funny: the green and yellow-tinted ones remind me of Herb's toilet. He never flushes, no matter how much I yell. His john's crappy."

His friend scratched an arm, looking interested and sympathetic. Watching a robin dislodging a stubborn worm, they pondered worm sizes; each inquired after the other's skill at fishing. Said One, contemplatively: "In my experience, worms in places like this get pretty big. I help Dad find ginormous ones in my granddad's dirt pile. He gets his kicks fishing, so I go along to keep him jollied, but it's way boring standing around fishing, or baiting hooks. I get majorly hungry. ...Caught a carp once, though. The best part is we always eat out afterwards, and my dad pays. He tells great jokes, and I mostly beat him at pool...

"Didjaknow flowers can kill, or, you can eat 'em? It depends. My granddad knows radical stuff like that." (He scanned the garden slowly.) "I don't see any killer flowers here... He's too old now to weed, so I do it, and he flips me a Jackson. I like splitting a beer with him, mostly."

They rose carefully from the bench, making crucial adjustments to their garb as they padded into the Ram's Head Garden. I heard Two say loudly, "Hey Jake, there's some stuffed cats in this library window, and they got a patio about the size of Cindy's bikini—Yo! Check out this statue! The poor geek's got buffalo legs! Bummer! Cin would freak." (Loud laughter.)

Gradually their voices faded, until I heard whoops; they'd come upon the surprise in the Brick-Walled Garden. I went slowly into the house, grinning, and breathing easier. They'd miraculously managed to traverse the entire garden with their low-rider pseudo-pants still hanging on.

Both teens had really looked, seeing things many people miss. Voice One knew quite a bit about complicated plants, and didn't feel silly saying so.

Under those casual, flippant commentaries, I mused, lurked a budding gardener.

A Gremlin Plague

HOUSE GREMLINS HAVE ALWAYS been a baffling part of my life. That pen I laid on the tabletop, right there, couldn't wander off. I'd just set it down, left briefly to fetch a pad, and come back to find the thing gone. Now I stand there, mouth open, catching flies, unable to process the simple fact that the pen. isn't. there. I retrace my steps, back to where the pads are, but of course I find nothing. I knew I wouldn't. I inspect my pockets, and the floor. Nothing.

Gremlins.

I conduct a really meticulous search. Nada. At last, having wasted 15 minutes, I give up and fetch another pen, but find myself so unnerved that I can't remember why I needed one in the first place.

The loss itches, like a mosquito bite. I nibble my nails, trying to work out what happened.

Two weeks later, that pen is still gone.

I do know the difference between gremlin interference and my own idiocy. The other day I prepared to bike to the library. I crammed books into my backpack and went to pick up my sunglasses. They'd vanished. I searched the house, and at last had to admit they'd probably been tipped into the trash.

I do that. Two portable phones, to date, have been set temporarily atop flower debris. I'll tote the heavy bucket to the alley bin, then absently tip in the lot and wander off. Much later I'll realize I have no phone. Using my cell, I'll run around the garden, repeat-dialing and listening. It'll ring faintly, choked by rubbish.

Anyway, at the library I ran a hand through my hair, only to discover my sunglasses perched jauntily on top of my head. A loud groan caused a lady to look at me, concerned. I felt like a perfect fool.

Gremlins have nothing to do with these situations. Gremlins are bolder, and much more unnerving.

On my knees in the garden I reached for my pruners—they'd gone. One minute before, they had been firmly seated in their leather holster. I searched, but in vain.

Here's the kicker. Five minutes later the holster, firmly clipped to my belt, had gone, too. Eight weeks later both are still hostage to garden gremlins, who certainly snicker just out of sight. Pruners and pouch will probably turn up in late fall, when I rake out the beds; even really resourceful gremlins find it hard to stash such substantial objects forever. Meantime, I'm reduced to using scissors. And bad language.

I won't even try to make you guess how many left-handed gloves have gone missing. I'll remove one briefly. When I reach for it, nothing. The workshop is littered with right-handed gloves. (Last fall I found four lefties in a spot I'd searched before, of course.)

Once, my mother, who had to put up with particularly obnoxious gremlins, baked and decorated a birthday cake. It vanished.

It's still gone, fifty years later. They'd probably eaten it. Now that's bold.

My (Irish) husband had his ring of important keys—er—shifted. We've just found them stuffed behind an ancient tennis racket in the garage, exactly six months later. We were struck dumb.
Gremlins.

The only time they've left us in peace was when we visited Ireland, in 1973. They'd vacationed, rejoining us at Shannon Airport. Never mind how I knew.

My thatch is thinner from pulling it in exasperation at their irritating sense of fun.

When Two Worlds Gently Bump

SOMETIMES INTERESTING CONNECTIONS HAPPEN in the garden. In late September, two fascinating men happened to sit down on the big garden bench at the same time. The first defined the proverbial "hayseed." He wore gray, faded overalls; a been-there baseball cap; sturdy, ancient lace-up boots; and a short-sleeved T-shirt that accommodated his generous belly and meaty arms. His face sported bristly whiskers perhaps two days old, but he was clean. (My hardworking Uncle Irvin, a dairy farmer, looked like that. He would round up his sleepy cows early every morning for milking, while I'd watch, fascinated, from the high fence.)

The other guy was exactly the opposite. He gleamed, so polished I needed sunglasses to gaze at his presentation. His Gucci loafers were rich, dark mirrors; his suit, a black-blue color cut in the European style, hung perfectly on a slim frame. Wrinkles wouldn't dare. He reminded me of how the awesome Anthony Hopkins dressed in my nearly all-time-favorite film, *Meet Joe Black*. (The original title was *Death Takes a Holiday*. That name change still irks me.)

They eyed each other curiously. Mr. Slim seemed a little unsure about whether to open a conversation, but the other guy looked genial. He smiled and said, "...Just what I need to finish a busy day. It's peaceful here; no phones ring, nobody needs me."

Mr. Hayseed nodded. "Yeah. I was turnin' manure, but the wife wanted to come to town to the farmer's market. She gets a kick out of squeezin' other people's veggies. What's your line?"

"Oh, I'm running a seminar at the Grand Traverse Resort; I have an office in downtown Detroit, and every year division heads meet up here to discuss various problems and solutions... boring, but a golf game eases the pain."

Mr. Casual chewed on that for a while, nodding. "Yeah, I like to bail rainwater out the old skiff, and row to a quiet spot an' drop me a line in. No one bothers me out there, cept' maybe 'skeeters, and I jes' brush 'em off, like you do with buzzin' juniors, I s'ppose."

Mr. Slim laughed appreciatively, and nodded. "You look comfortable. I miss wearing my jeans, but they'd certainly ruin my image. Home always looks good after these sessions."

Mr. Casual eyed the executive's garb, then patted his baggy overalls. "Hell, I'd have tractor-sized holes in them knees in a minute. I gotta have heavy-duty duds—tough gear for rough jobs..." He chuckled. "The last time I wore a fancy outfit was at our weddin' thirty-five years ago."

Slim grinned, gazing at the garden, deeply sniffing delectable scents. Then, suddenly inspired, he asked, "Hey, do you know a good restaurant on the way back I could try? For some reason, I feel like eating away from my crowd."

Without hesitation, the whiskered farmer said, "Mabel's. They serve up a tasty liver an' onions platter, mashed potatoes, gravy an' coleslaw.

Git their apple dumplin' dessert. You'll roll outta there happy as a pig in poop."

Directions were given, they shook hands, and Slim left with a spring in his step. He looked hungry.

The farmer settled back, grinning at me, grooming the geraniums behind him. "I'm real glad I followed my daddy's advice: 'Farmin's fine, suits won't suit; outside you'll shine, inside you'll whine.' He was right. I like bein' out, workin' machinery, tendin' livestock, not sittin' around tables, workin' my jaw."

Wiping grubby hands on my frayed, junk-stuffed cargo pants, I nodded happily; we were kindred spirits.

Wormy Halloween Thoughts

HALLOWEEN ALWAYS BRINGS OUT the imp in me. My usual witch costume always makes the little ones' eyes pop. With fingers in mouths they stare at the tiny, ancient, cackling hag as she rattles off Bach on her miniature organ. This presentation always goes over well, but I find myself needing a change. I finger ridiculous costumes, imagining myself as a lip-curling, squint-eyed, cigar-chomping, and distinctly abbreviated Clint Eastwood. Or maybe a giant, glittering, ravenous Japanese beetle, like those I battled all summer long. Or—GOT IT! I'll be a bookworm! Egad! My absurd-o-meter is dinging frantically! What fun! Becoming a worm rings my chimes!

Hmmm…I could slither into a flexible tube, the sort building-bashers dangle from second-story windows to funnel out rubbish. And I just happen to have elbow-length, silky black gloves, perfect for wormy arms to firmly grasp a good book. (They're left over from when I became a teeter-heeled, breathy, admittedly elderly Marilyn Monroe for one of Joe's birthday parties). What book? How about *The Secret Garden*… or maybe the classic scientific and satirical journal, the *Worm Runner's Digest*. I'll add granny glasses, and of course, my long-dead straw hat.

True art lies in the Dee-tails. I'll attach jiggly gummy worms to my hat, then pull 'em off to eat if I get hungry. That'll gross out, and delight, the kids.

Flexi-tubes, usually a disgusting off-white color, would press down into a manageable flatness for storage till the big night; more gummy worms could dangle from my rotund, larval main frame, too. I love it. I'm grubby most of the time, anyway, so this idea works, because it suggests, subtly, you understand, a tiny truth about moi.

Happy bookworms need to sit, and be comfortable. I can't stand around on the porch for three hours, perch-less. I'll dump my usual rocker (rocking worms are absurd) and cover my favorite overstuffed, comfy armchair with a black sheet, in Halloween's honor.

How about stacks of books surrounding the worm? I certainly have those…but then they'd have to be humped out of the library, onto the porch, and back inside again three hours later. I know! I'll plaster exterior walls with book-y wallpaper! I have just the thing, left over from the cat-crowded library window we created in the garden. I should include a very small bookcase, I suppose, stuffed with eye-popping adventure stories. Our library spilleth over with those.

Another thing. Bookworms require a library ladder to add ambience, and to munch, if they get bored. It's gotta have books on every rung—and, I'll need a smallish library desk, illuminated by an old brass lamp, of course.

Wait! I'm not done. A proper library needs a cat and a carpet, Shakespeare's mug, and the odd framed picture or two. I just happen to have the famous painting *The Bookworm*, and a portrait of kids reading something riveting. As for the treats, I'll "trashcan" them next to the desk.

The geek in me can't resist such a thoughtful, outrageous tableau. And thirty years out of the classroom, the teacher in me likes it too. Draculas, Dalmatians, the dreadful dead, and hungry hobos could do worse than devour a book. The best part? My worm outfit would certainly accommodate warm clothes.

Would she really do this? you wonder. Yup, I just might, if it's not raining or windy. The only way to find out for sure is to haunt my porch on Halloween. You'll know it's me because I'll be tunneling my way through a Honeycrisp apple while devouring a choice book—the very definition of bookwormy bliss.

Addendum: I wound up winding a king-sized down comforter around my person, then binding it with a spiral of duct tape. Excepting the stray feather, I think I had everyone convinced.

Odd Duck, Mish-Mash Thoughts

A drop of ink may make a million think. —Lord Byron

SOMETIMES GARDEN VISITORS LOOK at me sideways, not sure what to make of me. I mean, would you invite a gardener to dinner who has unmentionable and seemingly permanent muck beneath her fingernails? How many old ladies absently store worms in their hat brims to save them being killed? With odd-duck people, anything might happen. Sometimes I'll forget myself and discuss the musical transition from F major to D-flat major with my hose, which is often wielded in conducting motions as I work out rhythms knocking around in my noggin. My idea of fun grows forests of raised eyebrows.

As a child, I was a dreamer. Adventure books, *National Geographic* magazines, and a terrific rubber saddle that fit snugly onto my bike seat (sent away for with gum wrappers and two bucks) were treasures. I was more content in the worlds that Roy Rogers and the Black Stallion represented. Makeup, plucked eyebrows, face creams and other beauty enhancements bored me; why fix what ain't broke yet? Only older people needed lube and paint jobs. I was young. I thought blood-red lips and nails macabre. Still do.

My constant attraction to anything and everything printed tended to isolate me from regular girl stuff. Good at sports, I could hit balls reliably, pitch well, or run to win, but I rarely wanted to. Overnights in other kids' homes didn't appeal to me. As someone once said, "She keeps herself to herself." Yep. The thing is, I frequently disagreed, especially with adults, about important things, but had learned to keep silent. It wasn't proper for females to debate issues. Questions—especially in class, and especially from girls—were viewed as challenging authority. Why this should be a bad thing mystified me.

Best to keep low, and grow up. Then I'd be master of me.

Moving through childhood alone, I was free to investigate stuff at my own pace. One elderly librarian in our huge, gorgeous city library loved to chat with me, and expound on how books preserve experiences, insights and knowledge. No question I asked was stupid. But she was the exception.

Books transported me to amazing places. I'd fall asleep every night full of questions about knights, bug habits, anything to do with classical architecture, or the planets and constellations. I watched Roy Rogers gallop to the rescue for thirty thrilling minutes every Sunday at Gran's house, and always joined him in singing "Happy Trails to You" at the end. I saw four movies in my first thirteen years that made a lasting impression. *Fantasia's* stunning music and pictorial accompaniment led to avid reading about Earth's evolution; *My Friend Flicka*, with Roddy McDowall, left me paralyzed with wonder, as did *So Dear to My Heart* about a boy, his lamb, and a racehorse. I thrived on the thrilling radio stories of "The Shadow" and "Sky King."

The fire in *Bambi* seared me. I still can't watch that film.

I think the world is odd and mysterious and too predictable and utterly unpredictable. I love to tread the thin ice of scientific uncertainties, to ruminate over why pigs like truffles and cows don't. I hold my breath as scientists in Switzerland attempt cutting-edge, speed-of-light experiments with particle physics. I love to read about platypuses, and plantar's warts, cabbages and kings. My book diet is a weird smorgasbord.

Tonight a nice fire, a snug armchair, and *Odd Thomas*, author Dean Koontz's weird and wonderful creation, with a good cuppa and a gummy worm, are my prescription for contentment.

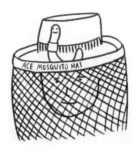

Unwashed, Unschooled, Unrivaled Genius

RECENTLY, I HOPPED ON MY ancient bike and pedaled to my own personal cathedral. Only a few blocks away, on the magnificent wooded grounds of the former mental hospital, stands a towering forest of giant evergreen trees. They were planted, I think, by the prescient Dr. Munson, who believed beauty would help to heal broken minds. Their trunks border a cathedral-wide pillared avenue that seems to go on forever. Over the past century, these mighty trees have sheltered and nurtured hundreds of sturdy seedlings now growing confidently to adulthood beside their parents. A thick bewilderment of branches muffle Division Street's traffic noises. The forest floor, with its deep carpet of pine cones and needles, feels springy under my feet. I walk my bike reverently, taking in the massive dignity with awe, while breathing in a century's accumulation of pungent perfume. (I am reminded of incense, damp, ancient stone, and candle wax.) The air is fresh. Sunlight emits a golden glow at the distant end of this long, towering tunnel. Slivers of November sky peep through the tops of seventy-foot-high branches. As with cathedrals, it's always cool here, even on hot summer afternoons. Little snow could find its way down to the forest floor, I muse.

Pausing, I lean my metal steed against a tree, and settle against its huge trunk to reflect awhile on the medieval minds that conceived and built Hereford, Gloucester, and Canterbury Cathedrals, to name a few. After a time away from those incredible structures I always find myself longing to return there, to breathe in genius. This place is as close to their awe-inspiring beauty as I can find. How lucky I am to live so near.

Think about it. The vast majority of uneducated men who dedicated their lives to raising the cathedrals didn't understand basic hygiene; herbs were all they had to help them cope with disease. Life spans then were brief; death and crippling injuries were constant companions. Rotten or inadequate food, severe winters, and marauding invaders were common nightmares.

They had to make every bit of clothing and equipment, like scaffolds and ladders and ropes and hammers. Paper was precious; architects would chisel intersecting lines onto the cathedrals' stone floors to visualize vital geometry.

Yet, they persevered. Those gigantic, glorious structures, conceived and erected a thousand years ago, still stand, astounding anyone not made of stone. Today, with all our computers, all our fancy tools, we can't do it. Look around. Nothing compares. Nothing ever will again. Barefoot men quarried millions of tons of magnificent stones; climbed dizzying heights; and created unrivaled, story-telling stained glass windows and statuary, which they raised to the heavens with the crudest handmade pulleys and which fit precisely. Each building, full of grace and towering strength, speaks eloquently of their unshakable faith more clearly than words ever could.

This wonderful pine forest recalls cathedral wonders in a much more intimate way. Sometimes, when the world is too much with me, a visit to the evergreen cathedral is my prescription for melancholy. What had seemed a pressing worry before is gently smoothed and sorted. Reorienting, I mentally zoom into space above Earth, and look down; everyday problems become less weighty, relatively unimportant in the Grand Scheme of Things. I empty my tangled thoughts, then refocus on accomplishments, beauty, simple joys, and the realization that I am part of it all, alive, connected.

The perfumed, peaceful silence, pierced by the clear call of a bird, follows me cheerfully as I pedal home through a thick, scattered, golden carpet of leaves with a much lighter heart.

Flakes, Felines, and Field Mice

IT WAS LATE NOVEMBER. The steady pitter-patter of rain and sleet lulled me. Toward first light, a hush settled, and I knew. Snow! I thumped downstairs, dressed in a flash, and dashed outside. Oh! An ocean of fat flakes fluttered down, teased into aerobatics by winds before they landed on the still-warm ground. In the fading moonlight the sedums' tops, my steel spider webs, and the long, slim blades of the giant miscanthus grasses sparkled. I tried to trap snowflakes on a red napkin to admire their exquisite architecture, but they'd always wink out too soon.

The sun slept late, then took the day off. Cheeky clouds took over. Gray-faced and bloated with moisture, they blew winter into northern Michigan. Snow soon blurred the landscape, softening harsh edges. Cold-nosed, I watched.

A young squirrel cautiously felt his way onto the lawn, intrigued by this radically different, whitened world.

Cat strolled across the alley, doing a curious dance. Every few steps he'd shake his footpads free of sticky snow, his annoyance plain. These silly paw-pauses made his journey longer than necessary. I couldn't help it—I laughed. Insulted, he flattened his tattered ears and stalked off, hind legs shooting out at odd angles, snow-wet fur rumpled. Not one of his better exits. Atop the fence, the sugar-frosted Chippie mocked the cat, his "chip-chip" of defiance clearly audible to the elderly feline, who gritted his ground-down teeth and soldiered on.

Old age ain't for sissies.

A car chugged slowly down the alley, decorated by a large, long-eared brown dog dangling from the front window, nose twitching, tongue hung loose as he contemplated pouncing on that cat. I heard a firm "Sam—NO" from his mind-reading master. The dog sagged slightly, but his hungry eyes remained locked on Cat's retreating back as he fantasized a different ending. Lacy flakes fell on his wet nose, dissolving instantly. The top of his snow-furred head suggested an old duffer remembering his youthful days, when hot pursuit was automatic.

Shrugging on my trusty backpack crammed with books, I trotted to the library for a refill. This walk is always enjoyable. But today, as I trundled across the rapidly vanishing grass path just before the train station, it moved! Someone was snow-tunneling, just ahead of my route! Exposed by my inquisitive boot, a horrified field mouse squeaked in alarm and fled into taller weeds. It shot one fearful glance at the sky; airborne death by hawk or owl was surely responsible for this traumatic near-hit. I felt a stab of guilt. No harm done, though.

Delicious sniffs from the EuroStop Café made my nose twitch as I stepped over multiple train tracks and trudged toward the library's entrance. I would probably indulge in lunch there on the way back.

Two plump gray rabbits hopped unhurriedly by, heading toward the library's Children's Garden, which serves as a rabbit restaurant and lodging house all winter long. They barely acknowledged me. (*The Story of Peter Rabbit*, with its charming sketches, might be a book to revisit, I mused.)

The animal world, right under our insensitive noses, was thriving.

Flashing Spock's "live long and prosper" greeting to all, I settled into the library's treasures, ignored by Traverse City's feathered and furry folk. Though I recall that mice occasionally enjoy devouring a good book, too.

The Glums, Mr. Grinch, and Simple Gifts

SUDDENLY, THE HOLIDAYS ARE HERE. This year, offering gifts to those we cherish can be a challenge, as wallets are thin, smiles are elusive, and nails and tempers are distinctly shorter.

But I'm rediscovering the power to savor, and offer, less tangible gifts—with no pain.

In this unnerving economic atmosphere I've tried to take stock of simpler, personal realities. I'm healthy, warm, dry, fed, loved, and—this is important—I own a mirror. It's been moved into the kitchen to remind me of the importance of laughter.

That mirror reflects my eyes, the essence of me. The trick is to get smiles to travel from my mouth to that higher level. The mirror clearly sees that the eyes have it—the sparkle of rich, hearty humor. It's good to be alive.

When I get the Glums, when optimism seems elusive, I'll reflect on the Grinch, and really laugh! How could I not chuckle, recalling that outrageous rogue's silly antics as he efficiently steals simply everything from 'Who' villagers, but discovers something simply wonderful, instead. (Boris Karloff was an inspired choice for the personification—the voice and soul—of Mr. Grinch (from Dr. Seuss's delightful book, *How The Grinch Stole Christmas*). I'll recall that sly, wonderful song, and the Grinch's leer, that absurd hat and those l-o-n-g fingers, then toss in the image of his obsequious, put-upon mutt wearing those dopey antlers—and BOOM! Belly-laughter happens, as reliably as Yellowstone's Old Faithful geyser, doggone it. Pounds of worry and distress fall away.

So many delights are free. I can give hugs to people I love, and shamelessly lick the bowl of whipped cream I've made to top off my bumpkin pie (my childhood name for that treat). I'll savor the unique aroma of fresh-ground coffee, and set the table using the charming laminated drawings created by schoolchildren who've visited my garden. I can hold close the memory of my mother's smile as she opened homemade prezzies, and enjoy the sight of young children gaping at a food-laden holiday dinner table, or at the exquisite lights decorating snow-trimmed trees in downtown Traverse City. These are free joys, and they're all around me.

Yesterday I opened one of Gary Larson's hilarious *Far Side* cartoon books. Three spectacled chickens in a restaurant bathroom were trying to apply lipstick. "It's no use, Wanda," one sighs. "Like they say—we just don't have lips..." It's impossible to remain, er, broody. (Ha! Aren't words delicious?)

I can't resist a yummy peanut butter-and-white chocolate chunk cookie from Poppycock's, or the cheerful grin of a tired waitress, or the amazing sight of hundreds of hats, thousands of hats, millions and billions and trillions of hats in Diversions, that fascinating downtown Traverse City store.

I love visiting the Park Place Hotel's wonderful little shop, Anna's Creations and Collectibles, to explore its endless, intriguing, affordable gift ideas. The proprietors are delightful.

My oven has the power to tantalize noses and tastebuds. Homemade zucchini bread, cookies, pies and such make wonderful gifts. Who wouldn't be touched by tummy-love? Recycled Easter baskets stuffed with simple culinary delights, and perhaps a tucked-in, store-bought, exactly right treasure, make smiles sparkle.

The enlightened Mr. Grinch, who reminds me to remember what's important, celebrated the season with all those thankful, hardworking Whos, who cherished, and happily shared, the gifts of simplicity, laughter and joy.

The rest simply didn't matter.

Odd Birds

My own suspicion is that the universe is not only queerer than we suppose, but queerer than we can suppose. —J. B. S. Haldane

MY LATE FRIEND BETTY OWNED a parrot, Hank, who'd been part of her family for over fifty years. Once she read a pundit's political opinion aloud to her husband. Hank sighed and said, "Not politics. Can we avoid this minefield?" Betty, used to potshots from parrots on perches, told him to hush, which really annoyed the bird. "You want brush-offs? I can do that." He turned his back on her, muttering epithets. He had been raised by a sailor, and his, er, colorfowl vocabulary sometimes got out of hand.

When visiting Betty's house, I'd feel the brunt of Hank's wit. One day he eyed me and said "Looking a little fat, aren't we?" He cackled. If I ventured to make a comment, he would glare, and sometimes deign to reply, or more often chastise.

When Betty died, the old bird went silent.

Years later, settled into my rumpled, overstuffed chair parked by the fire, I opened my e-mail and discovered a fascinating video sent along by my cousin, featuring Snowball, someone's white cockatoo. A sofa's dark rim showed him off beautifully as he squawked and danced, in perfect rhythm, to the infectious music of the Backstreet Boys. John Travolta would be jealous; Patrick Swayze would unhesitatingly swap his partner for this splendid bird's perfect agility. Clawed feet were flung out as he displayed extra-fancy footwork. His body bobbed, and his considerable crest rose and fell to the beat. When the last note finished, he accepted congratulations from applauding family, taking multiple, crest-flinging bows.

I sat back, flabbergasted.

Earlier that year, at Thanksgiving, I had pushed open the heavy garage door that led into the garden, then staggered down the slippery sidewalk toward the back door with weighty grocery bags banging against my legs, when SMACK! Something large (and soft, thank heaven) hit my left shoulder, and fell, plop, onto the path beside me. What on earth?! I set down the heavy bags, and stared in confusion. The still-warm, perfect body of a pigeon lay before me. The wings were splayed out, revealing soft blue and gray feathers, liberally splashed with white. On his back, the bird's orange feet reached for the sky. Gorgeous, I thought, as I rubbed my aching shoulder.

Here's the thing: he was curiously unbloodied—but headless. I squinted up at the muddy sky. Nothing but air. No larger bird, no branches, just this pigeon, minus his thinker.

Stumped, I stood there, brooding. I hadn't noticed any pigeons with mental problems lately. No children with slingshots were near. I finally decided that a hawk must have dispatched him high up in the icy air, then gobbled his dead head before absentmindedly releasing the body.

Hmm. Three inches to the right and I would have been bird-brained. (Here's a disconcerting thought. I recalled Gary Larson's cartoon of a bird looking down at a human, imagining a target painted on the guy's bald head. The caption read "A bird's-eye view" or something to that effect. I was toting a fat, decidedly dead turkey. Maybe a disgruntled falcon or hawk, not thrilled about the holiday season, had decided to make a point.)

Sadly, I removed the heavy body to the trash, then trudged into the house, reflecting that the poor beast probably never knew what had happened. But why hadn't its attacker finished the meal? It can't be easy to pounce on a large pigeon in mid-flight, and nature's never wasteful. After writing about this in the newspaper a week later, I received a note about it from a reader. She had spotted a hawk in her yard, dining on a pigeon's head.

What are the odds?!

Snowed Rodents and White Art

WHAT A SIGHT! WINTER HAS arrived, and my huge fountain is buried. If I didn't know better, I'd think there was nothing there. Wind-sculptured snow has blanketed the sides of the fountain's slanted, tarp-wrapped boards, disguising its shape; the whole thing has vanished into a white-on-white canvas.

Bundled up, I trotted outside to shovel the front porch and sidewalk, then stood quietly, listening. Snow had smothered the normal city sounds; enveloped in cotton batting, the world was thick with silence. That made it easy to pick out the scratch of claws-on-bark, nearby. A black squirrel made his way down the side of a venerable maple tree. He studied the snow for a few seconds from about seven feet up, then, skipping the last yard or so of trunk, he jumped. Ker-plop! Poof! Awk! The bewildered rodent vanished into a deep drift. He'd miscalculated!

I heard a shocked, but muffled, exclamation, and laughed out loud. This was obviously a young, inexperienced squirrel. Gathering himself, he made a mighty leap out—poof! He vanished again! From a distance the sight was hilarious; the frazzled rodent bounced in and out of deep powder, then completely disappeared after every enormous leap. Finally, he made it to another sturdy trunk about ten yards away. Snow outlined his long whiskers, and clung to his bushy tail.

After a good shake, he climbed to a lower branch to consider things. Huh. This was a very different world.

Another black squirrel descended the same naked maple; they stood, nose-to-nose, and commiserated. I mean, those two discussed the situation. I heard little chitter-noises, magnified by the silence, as they tried to figure out where their stashes were—the topography had utterly changed. Their bellies were impatient. What to do? They remained together for a long time, exchanging ideas. Getting cold, I grabbed my backpack from the front doorknob and walked to the grocery, grinning.

When I got back, it began to snow again. The squirrels had vanished, but there were deep pockets in the snow leading toward the huge blue spruce. That journey must have been exhausting.

I climbed the stairs to the front door, noting tracks on the porch floor that led to the covered furniture around the corner. Hmmm. Someone was camping out under the porch furniture covers. Less wind blew there; the snow wasn't as deep. I recalled the river of cats I'd disturbed last winter; they'd established a hostel of sorts there. But this was just one set of tracks. I'd seen a possum sniffing around about 4 days earlier—surely not. And please, don't let it be a skunk! (I'd gotten a nauseating whiff before first light yesterday, as I'd ventured outside to grab the paper.)

Suddenly I had an idea. Everyone else had made their mark in those pristine piles of fluff. Now it was my turn.

Carefully moving through the deep drifts to an unblemished spot, I positioned myself stick-straight, then fell backward, arms at my side. Poof! Now I was flat, practically invisible, and ready. I scissored my arms and legs back and forth, back and forth, wind-blown snow spraying my face; I could feel it redden with cold. Done! I rose, carefully, and looked. Aha! A perfect angel! Childhood skills remained happily intact. My grin widened.

Wait a minute! Anyone could have created this art. Hmmm. To dispel any doubt, I signed my name with a snowy flourish!

Unimpressed, Mama Nature quietly erased all our "Kilroys" within an hour.

Magic Fingers, Marvelous Evening

JOE AND I ZIPPED INTO Chicago recently to spend a concert evening with Australian Tommy Emmanuel, "a certified guitar player." This classic "Tommy" humor was on the ticket stub. Huh. The guy is simply the most amazing guitarist in the world, that's all. My eyes were on stalks! He did impossible things, to thunderous cheers. Though I knew what I'd witness, I was overwhelmed. We sat at tables, sipping drinks; dumbfounded first-timers in the packed auditorium gasped and performed classic ohm'god motions, and more than one beverage was spilled. We felt our hair blow backward, like the famous poster of the guy in his armchair listening to the great sound that blows him away—remember? Tommy is his own band. His sound is incredible.

To warm up the crowd, another Aussie, Anthony Snape, played. Wow! He sang like an angel, exhibiting a huge vocal range and great guitar work. He writes his own stuff. One song called "Still not over you" stood out. Anthony is very young, in his mid-twenties; last year, a total unknown, he sent his newly minted CD to Tommy, and held his breath—for about a millisecond. No way would "The Great One" ring him. But, by golly, Tommy did. In fact, he invited Anthony to come to America with him and open every concert. Typical. He's generous to fresh young musicians, and does his best to help them on to fame. Here, we have a genuinely decent human being.

In his mid-50s, tall, slim, agile Tommy is happy in his own skin. The audience feels connected immediately; he's appreciative of our responses, and doesn't mind chatting about his family, and meaningful events in his life, like final jam sessions with his dying hero, Chet Atkins.

He told us about an Aussie man named Jack, who never missed any of Tommy's fifty-nine Australian concerts. His happy face had become a fixture. When he was diagnosed with terminal cancer, his family wrote and explained why he wouldn't attend again. So, Tommy visited Jack at his modest home. Bedridden, overcome with joy, Jack presented him with a 1930s $49 Sears Roebuck guitar, pristine, still in its case. (Tommy brought it out to show us; it was smallish, plain, unimpressive. But Ohh! In his hands that instrument sang.) Jack, thrilled to hear it played at his bedside, died very shortly after, a happy man.

Tommy loves that cheap guitar.

Three offerings will stay with me forever. Tommy used one of his four guitars as a sound board—a drum, actually, for the most amazing display of technique I've ever witnessed. It was worn nearly through from his hands-on magic. No actual notes were played until nearly the end—just rhythm as I've never heard it, ever. It's impossible to adequately convey what he does. It has to be seen and heard to be believed. By the way, though it looked exhausted, that instrument had a lovely voice. Tommy called it "broken in."

Two other songs brought tears. The first was an exquisite, shimmering guitar rendering of "Over the Rainbow"; the other, about missing his dad, was called "I Still Can't Say Goodbye." His pure, almost choirboy-like tenor voice soared; his poetry was simple, and stunning.

Tommy loves people, and loves sharing his music. The audience felt honored to witness his artistry. If you ever have the chance to attend a concert, go. Bring a drool rag. Warning! You'll either chuck your guitar right then, or want to practice with dedicated intensity for years.

We left with huge grins, grateful to have ears.

Lilliputian View of an Alien World

TODAY, IN THE FAIRY GARDEN, I've decided to lie on my belly and look around. Dirt-y thoughts crawl through my head. For example, which end of a worm is the one I should watch? I've pondered profundities like this for years. And why do worms often sun themselves atop the Irish moss? They are signature dinners for opportunistic robins, but undaunted, they'll lie there quietly, thinking thoughts... Worms belong below stairs, but they frequently disagree with me on that point.

Down amid the corydalis and Labrador violets is more fascinating stuff—better than TV, any day. How many times have I watched the vigorous tug-of-war between robin and worm? How does the creature resist? He's slippery, and should slide like butter into that lethal beak, but no. Worm manages to brace himself; the robin must fight for every bite. Amazing. These robust, rubbery, string-bean creatures represent an alien world.

When I was young I'd dash outside after a downpour to rescue soaked worms that writhed helplessly on our sidewalk. They seem clueless about the dangers of drenching rains; why haven't they evolved a plan to avoid this frequent calamity? You'd think armies of waterlogged, coughing worms would make an impression on the rest. Maybe they can't remember which end of themselves harbors the wit to work out this perennial problem.

A millipede, carefully disentangling one of its zillion legs from a moss blossom, finds traveling over those minute flowers a challenge. (How in the world does it manage so many feet?)

But, for hilarity, I poke pill bugs. They like to bustle about, eating, socializing, making more pill bugs, burrowing under all manner of damp and rotting material. When I flip over a rock while neatening, there is general consternation. Everyone scrambles for cover, or rolls up and waits, hoping for the best, I suppose. God-like, I can touch one gently, and it immediately rolls into itself, like a donut without a hole. If I push it, as I would a bowling ball, it'll roll dizzily along the bricks— Wait! Does a pill bug get dizzy?

These creatures have left fossil imprints of lives lived eons ago; not much has changed regarding design. (If it ain't broke…)

But ants have my deep respect. "Lazy" isn't part of their vocabulary. They are born knowing their jobs; they possess the strength of giants. Their homes are elaborate, and future generations are looked after with fanatical dedication. They even capture and milk aphids for sweet treats. These slaves are protected, and probably can imagine a worse fate than being "down under" with their ant-tagonists.

I've seen ants give the "high-five" to their fellows; antennas bump together, essential news is exchanged, but no time is wasted gossiping. Ants epitomize "industrious." Not one of their children is maladjusted. Instead, they are cherished, and do their jobs confidently, knowing they're essential to the colony's survival.

We find it impossible to distinguish one ant from another. Yet, if an absent-minded neighboring ant should forage into their territory, affronted "homeland" ants' noses always know; the invader will smell, well, wrong. Pounce! He'll be dead.

Here's another mystery. Chippie lives under this stone slab. Do ants bypass the snoring chipmunk, or do they crawl all over him at night when he's trying to sleep, having learned eons ago that he is no threat?

Come to think of it, do chipmunks get fleas?

As I lie here pondering, ants march up my pant leg, forcing me to "do the dance." Maybe there's a message here…

Bandits, Bees and Copycats

A GARDEN MIGHT SEEM BORING to outwardly mobile folks. They haven't lived at Sunnybank. Stuff happens here.

Last week I had a fountain-cleaning day. Birds love to dangle their backsides over the high, ornamental rim of the huge black bowl to poop into the pool below. This creates a lush green slime that coats the bottom of this romantic garden feature.

Groaning with the effort, my helper and I emptied the weighty basin, lowered its massive bulk to the ground, started the pool pump, mopped and scrubbed on hands and knees, then finally refilled the monster. But this time I added my latest anti-yuck additive—a fat cup of household bleach. It's worked wonderfully well. I can go nearly twice as long without cleaning. An occasional freshening now and then with another half-cup keeps it clear.

That night I woke with a start to hoarse murmurs and splashes in the main fountain. There were invader-waders, caring not a whit for stealth. I bolted downstairs to the kitchen window. A full moon revealed two well-fed raccoons playing in the pool, tweaking the aluminum swans' beaks. One drank, tentatively, then spat it out— phafft! Climbing out about five minutes later, they smoothed their fur, waddled across the grass to the tiny patio, lifted their bulky bums over the big fence, and vanished. Morning revealed no onerous deposits—only perfect, childlike handprints that were clearly visible on the pristine pool bottom. Observant visitors were fascinated.

I woke two mornings later about three A.M, made coffee, and sipped it outside on the back porch stairs. I was mosquito-veiled and invisible.

Operatic felines were tuning up in the moonlight. Yowling and hissing, a black one walked along the alley fence top, fur stylishly erect, tail stiff. But when he leaped down five feet into my lovely chocolate Eupatorium, I lost it! White granny gown billowing, face blurred by mesh, I leaped up with a squawk, galloped toward the beasts and tossed my cooled coffee, nailing one! Multiple cats exploded out of the foliage, shrieking, and roared up the fence and away, their battle abandoned.

I smirked: cats are rarely surprised by anything, but I'd scared the yowls right out of them. Bonus: one sozzled puss would experience a coffee-jolt when he tried to clean himself.

Yesterday I crawled under the big tree mallow to pluck out some fallen blossoms, when Bzzzt! A branch-bumped bee tumbled down the back of my neck and frantically six-footed it up and down my spine, under my shirt. Hollering, I snatched out my tucked tails, desperately trying to dislodge it. Seeing the light it zoomed down and out, too confused to sting; four startled visitors were treated to a spontaneous dance, a half-undone shirt and my high-pitched yelps. The shocked bee was much more dignified.

Recently, a very young child toured the garden with his parents. Thumb in mouth, he stared at the water streaming from the flute of the first fountain's little brass boy; mom had to tug to get him moving. The fairy fountain's kissing children, with a tiny stream of water emerging from under their feet, had his finger stabbing the air. "Angels!" he cried, struggling to get closer.

But the big fountain undid him. After staring intently at it for a minute he uncorked his thumb, pulled down his training pants and urinated into the pool. I froze. His shocked father gaped, completely undone. Mom stared at me, horrified, then whispered, "I am SO sorry!" She snatched him up, adjusting his tiny shorts: "Jerry, we don't do wee-wee here!"

The little guy, incredulous, pointed where he'd been. "But momma, they were!"

I still ache from laughing.

Two Kinds of Slime, and One Diamond

ONE SUMMER DAY ABOUT 6:00 A.M., Joe and I decided to take our small boat out onto the bay to test our new propane grill, which was specially designed for small craft. Suspended securely over the side, it's capable of cooking up to four thick, nicely seasoned hamburgers.

As we navigated the river early that morning gulls flew overhead, screaming, while silent geese at the mouth of the river floated serenely in a tight flock, ignoring our slow passage. The sun was still just hinting, and the Grand Traverse Resort's glass walls, piercing the sky so far away, shimmered in eerie, reflected morning light.

By unspoken agreement we continued our slow, no-wake progression after clearing the river mouth, unwilling to penetrate the silence with unnecessary noise. The boat purred along happily, seeming eager to abandon her moorings for a quiet adventure.

The water was black and calm, its surface reminiscent of a slightly puckered patchwork quilt. Suddenly, well out on the bay, this smoothed to flat, inky black. And, I noticed something odd. Just a foot below the surface a distinct layer of something suddenly appeared. One instant there was nothing, the next, this presence. I exclaimed, and we stopped to more closely examine it. Algae? Hmmm. I'd never seen such a massive, greenish-yellow, loosely connected blanket, which moved in perfect synchrony to the gently undulating water. Later the Record-Eagle assured folks the unusual accumulation wasn't harmful, and would soon dissipate. But yuck! I wouldn't dive into it.

All morning we stayed out there, enveloped in quiet, reading, watching the sunrise, and noting spooky bubbles rising mysteriously from beneath that vast, slimy blanket.

Voices traveled through the still air to our craft; they came from faraway people settling down on their patios for coffee and chat. Their words were melodic mush.

An exhausted hornet found us; she landed gratefully on a seat, and, after a rest, flew off, refreshed. It was a huge distance for the insect to manage, which triggered a discussion about the impossible reality of bumblebee flight. Nature is amazing.

We grilled mid-morning hamburgers, then happily putt-putted home three hours later, with me out on the bow watching that fascinating algae blanket cleanly split by our prow. Well before we hit the shallower water, it abruptly vanished. Fishermen casting their lines at the river's mouth, with no inkling of what lay out there, nodded good morning as we crawled past.

Days later, after a rain, we biked back to bilge the boat, and found it had been vandalized. Invaders had undone the canvas, entered, thrown the radio into the river and tossed things about. Fortunately, the locked cuddy cabin prevented worse damage. An abandoned mountain bike and beer cans tossed in the reeds nearby had probably been part of this. The police said our neighbor's bigger boat had also been hit, more severely.

Joe, donning a wetsuit, felt around the river bottom for the solid-state radio, hoping to salvage it. Muck and limp water grass clung to his hair and body; a not-unpleasant earthy odor replaced his aftershave. As he toweled dry the policeman commented that night patrols had been discontinued due to budget constraints, but he'd request random nighttime boat checks. Small comfort for river-berth folks.

Later, at home, upset and depressed, I wandered into the secret garden to find three children admiring water drops sparkling atop the Lady's Mantle. One youngster chuckled. "Wow! If these diamonds were real I could make lots of people happy…like my mom, f'instance…"

Knowing his mother already had her diamond, I laughed, much cheered.

Our Bray-zen Paddy MacDonk

MY FAMILY LIVED ON THE Isle of Skye for five years in the late 70s. My mother's delightful husband, David, tells this interesting story about an addition to the family.

"We were driving home from the tiny village of Portree one miserable, sleety, windy day," he said, "when Barbara grabbed my arm, shouting, "Stop the car, David!" There, standing alone in a field, was a soaking wet donkey. Icicles hung from his shaggy coat. His hooves were badly neglected, having grown long and curving, making it difficult to walk. The sight was shocking.

"Naturally, Barbara wanted to buy him. English friends Peter and Jean, who lived nearby, managed to locate the owner. Soon we had a phone number. The farmer was willing to sell him for forty pounds cash, including delivery. So Paddy MacDonk came into our lives.

"We knew absolutely nothing about donkey care. Our neighbour gave us good advice, and a rope halter.

"First, we called the vet to deal with those great, curved hooves. I haltered Paddy and stood by his head while the vet went to work with large clippers and a rasp. Paddy stood quietly during the whole, long operation. The vet, having attended him before, remarked that he was much easier to manage, now. We guessed that Paddy's former life had been grim.

"That donkey had a bray to rouse the dead. Hoarse, penetrating calls echoed through the fields, waking the sheep, shaming the rooster. It was impossible to sleep while he hee-hawed and gasped, in classic donkey style.

"While he was never nasty, he did show a wicked sense of humour. I'd built him a shelter, open on one side, to use during Skye's frequent, intense gales. One feeding time he followed me in and deliberately pressed me hard against the wall; it was difficult to breathe! Finally, after much pushing, I escaped. After that, I'd let him enter first.

"Another memorable time, while I measured out his breakfast, Paddy grabbed the middle finger of my left hand in those large, yellow front teeth, and held it; I could do nothing but stand there and endure, while he studied me thoughtfully. Finally I was released, with my finger miraculously intact, though it was sore for days.

"He was quite docile with the young daughter of the local police-man on his back. He'd join us on walks, too. Barbara, our two dogs, Fred and Charlie, Jinjii, our cat, and Paddy and I would often wander down to the ruined Duntulm Castle, causing locals to gawk from behind their curtains. Paddy got on well with our friendly Lab, Fred, but he hated our border collie, Charlie, who always tried to herd him. Once he landed a glancing kick; the shocked dog came to me with blood dripping from his mouth. I had a look; there was a perfect set of canine tooth marks on his tongue. From then on, Charlie kept well clear of his hooves.

"Paddy was a great favourite with tourists who hiked to house." (It was a little home-based clock shop and bed-and-breakfast.) "He'd trot to the fence, braying loudly, often winning an apple or carrot.

When he chose to display his 'manhood' there was much amazement, and possibly envy, too.

"We eventually moved back to England, and had to say goodbye. Happily, a well-known donkey sanctuary in the South of England agreed to take him. When they arrived, a mother and foal, rescued from further north in Scotland, were in the other horsebox. Paddy would have company during the long trip south."

So he passed out of their lives, having given them, and so many visitors, years of pleasure.

Encounters in a Parallel Dimension

MICHIGAN WEATHER IS NEVER DULL. We've received nearly three feet of snow; yet, when I peer through the window this outrageously early morning, everything out there is enveloped in a blanket of thick mist—and it's softly, almost invisibly, raining! Weird. So, naturally, I pick up my umbrella and pop out for a walk in the dark.

The swirling air is spooky. There is no sound; even the cars are asleep. Hannah Park is reduced to a series of vague shapes. The moon, copied by frosted street lamps, bathes everything in an unearthly, gleaming, icy halo, intricately highlighting black trees and shrubs. Structures gleam. I walk slowly, cleated boots biting into the slick snow, admiring the bright relief of lingering Christmas lights.

There comes the occasional quack, oddly muffled by the thick air as ducks, half asleep, note that they float in mystery. Maybe those quacks help everyone keep together, as ducky reference points have all but vanished. It's the moonlight zone.

Suddenly, shockingly, a sharp bullet-crack breaks the stillness. A largish branch has chosen now to give in to gravity. It crashes to the ground, shattering into pieces just in front of me, dying between the lawn and the sidewalk in front of the funeral home. Close, I muse, but no cigar. Fate has a lousy aim.

Just the same, wary now, I move to the middle of the all-white street. Tall walls of older, plow-heaved snow define its edges.

The dead of night is dead...Wait! Just ahead there's movement. Emerging from the mist stroll three fat bodies with bandit-markings. All three rear up and stare; clearly, I am the intruder here. These raccoons are annoyed, and totally unintimidated. I feel hot embarrassment, caught out like a trespasser or a Peeping Tom. Eyes skewer me. They don't move—they don't even blink. I hate this. I know what they're thinking. (What's she doing out here, wandering around in the dark, disturbing the peace? Humans are dimwits—too stupid to stay out of the weather.)

One masked beast is clutching a half-wrapped parcel of something edible. The papered item brings to mind fish-and-chips wrapped in newspaper, a favorite take-away in England. I've interrupted their shopping trip.

After a bit, I say tentatively, "Hello, there." It breaks the spell; they lower themselves to waddle slowly down into Hannah Park with their booty, dismissing me utterly.

Whose trash has been lightened? These guys are stealthy; I never heard them coming until they'd suddenly materialized in the street. "...Strangers in the night, exchanging glances..." Sinatra's voice winds around my neurons as I carry on, smiling.

There is another dimension that operates at night, in the Moonlight Zone; those who enter it risk a sort of enchantment. This parallel world operates at its own speed, experiencing its own triumphs and tragedies, ignored by, and invisible to, day-trotters. At 3:30 A.M. anything can happen, without benefit of batteries, or the wheel. In this dark world, the rules are different. Alien. Humans are irrelevant.

This softer, darker stratum smoothly adapts to civilization's changes, using human alterations to further its own ends. The lessons are simpler. Food is life; inattention invites death. Walk softly, look hard, run fast, grow claws. Learn.

Brown, careless mice stand out against white snow, serving owls. Raccoons know how to shop trash bins. Sleepy fish park safely in the river's deep middle. Cats slink delicately along snowy walks, intrigued by the menu choices.

I am a stranger in a strange land.

Washed-Out English Thoughts

IT'S 6 A.M. I'M SWATHED in layers of clothing, huddled next to a snapping kitchen fire, precariously balancing a large, ancient, much-thumbed atlas of the world on my knees while typing away on my laptop computer. I dine atop this book, too.

Fresh coffee, strong, rich, and black as the night, warms my cup and hands. British bacon and a small loaf of crusty brown bread go down well. I purchased them from the little shop in Wormelow Tump, down in the valley below.

Green England has a fresh, early-spring scent. When I open the door to reach for more firewood, flashes of white remind me that snow-drops are determinedly emerging from their cold beds to brighten our forest. Their perfect white heads poke through mountainous piles of drenched household debris—our beloved family cottage has experienced a massive flood.

Here's what happened. In mid-December the gardener, who manages the plant life here, appeared for his bi-monthly morning's work. Not seeing my stepfather David at the window as usual, he went into the unlocked house, where he found him collapsed on the bedroom floor. The ambulance was summoned, and before dashing away, its crew thoughtfully switched off the heat (as it made no sense to waste costly fuel). They then locked the cottage, and someone stored the labeled key in Hereford County Hospital's safe.

But these tiny, vital facts were lost in the confusion.

As David had no wallet on him, we weren't notified until Christmas Eve, a week later. By then, he was recovering nicely, but would remain hospitalized for some time. The house key's location was a worrying issue; no ER personnel seemed to know anything. Not certain the cottage was secure, I phoned the hospital daily for ten days to track it down. Finally, one clever soul (a hospital higher-up from Idaho, who'd married an English woman and emigrated) thought to check the hospital's safe. Bingo!

Joe and I planed an orderly visit in late January to ready the cottage for David. But (there's always a "but," isn't there? Life happens while we're making other plans) on December 26, England experienced an unusually prolonged freeze. All the attic pipes burst in the unheated cottage. Water poured from the ceilings for eleven days, sparing only the master bedroom and bath.

When Hospital Social Services did a routine house check, they were greeted by a river of water rushing down the walk. The mains were eventually located and turned off, but by then it was far too late. Ceilings had crashed to the floors. Upholstered furniture, handmade hooked rugs, precious books, desks, walls, carpets, pictures—everything—was awash. David was devastated.

We took the next red-eye to England.

What a mess. For two weeks we've waded through cold, ruined rooms, tossing and sorting. Insurance people buzz around, trying to figure out what can be saved and what's irretrievable. This process will continue for weeks, so I'll remain here, camping in the one tiny area not destroyed, to coordinate restoration efforts.

Bright spots? Yesterday I saw an inquisitive hedgehog poking around, snuffling noisily as it searched for bugs and worms.

The weather is damp and cool; I listen to Classic FM while peeling away soaked wallpaper and gulping endless, bracing cups of tea. I'll drive to Ross-on-Wye's Royal Hotel parking lot to steal two minutes of wireless internet connection to send columns to my editor and updates to family. David, still away, is mending. Things can be replaced. I'll just go with the flow.

Echh! I think I've had quite enough of that particular metaphor.

An English Teashop

Reminiscence

RECENTLY I HOSTED TWO long-time British friends. Chatting with them brought back the flavor of England, where I've spent many delightful days over the years, exploring historic Hereford and Ross-on-Wye, near my family's home in Herefordshire. Many ancient buildings there lean comfortably, their dignified timbers seemingly impervious to insects and time.

One cold day I went into a tiny teashop in the middle of Hereford's huge midtown square, which is reserved for pedestrians. It would be lovely to set down my groceries, rest my tired feet and enjoy a bracing cup of tea. Bundled people milled around outside, toting webbed shopping bags crammed with crusty loaves of bread, fresh veggies, and perhaps a "joint" for Sunday dinner. Sighing, I settled next to an ancient, stooped man, who was slurping his tea with obvious pleasure. His bright eyes scanned the square, never missing a thing. I often enjoy chats with strangers—it's frequently fascinating—and so I bade him good afternoon.

Turning to me with a smile, he said, "Tain't good 'til me sweet passes under me nose, young lady. What brings you hereabouts?"

I explained that I was visiting family, as I tried to do every year. He nodded.

"The States—too young to know any better, too brash to grasp what's important. Look around. What strikes?"

I immediately shot back, "The architecture. I never get enough of venerable English Gothic cathedrals, black-and-white timbered houses that Shakespeare saw, cobblestoned streets, centuries-old trees still thriving…but mostly the buildings. For me they sing. The English understand preservation."

"Aye; 'tis the Old World, you know." He grinned, and, startled, I saw his teeth in the palm of his hand. He'd removed them quietly, and his amusement at my discomfiture was clear.

"Haven't broken 'em in yet, m'dear. They're new, see, and I always enjoy how white me choppers are 'til a thousand cups of tea stains 'em brown. So I pops 'em out regular at teatime, 'til I forget. Everybody preserves everything here." He threw back his head and laughed.

Amused, I joined in. Clearly, this little joke had made his day. Then my tea and his scones, clotted cream and jam came; he expertly popped in his gleaming teeth and polished off the food.

Mr. Longworth told me he came to town weekly to visit his wife's grave, change the flowers, and "have a wander down memory lane." They'd been married fifty-eight years.

He'd dug his future wife out of the debris that had been her London home during the Blitz. Though she'd lost everything, she kept her sense of humor, joking as volunteers worked to free her that as long as her spectacles worked and she never missed teatime, all would be well. He'd also admired her brusque dismissal of her broken arm.

"She said the lads fighting the massive nightly fires were the ones to admire. She'd manage just fine, thank you very much." He sighed. "So, I married 'er. She liked my smile. My teeth were the first thing she saw under the flat's rubble as I bent down to pull 'er outa there. Teeth, spectacles and tea things…Funny what comes to mind when you've too much time to think."

Replete, he pushed away from the little table, paid for everything, and shook my hand firmly.

"I hope the world always remembers what's important, lassie: history's more 'n old buildings, or old people hanging on, like me. It's about spirit, and laughs, and warm digs with a great lady."

With a flash of white, an arched eyebrow and a chuckle, he capped his bald head, and slowly left the shop.

English Backbone

THE WORLD WAR II MEMORIES of the elderly English are vivid. Mr. Longworth and his friends still mourned those who had died, were burned, or had lost their homes in the horrific fires that ravaged London during the Blitz. When living in London in the seventies I could still find evidence of those massive fires; I was astonished that both Westminster Cathedral and St. Paul's had survived.

Firm friendships were forged underground, in London's subways, which served as bomb shelters. Deep within their cramped, makeshift accommodations, Londoners would wait for hours, or even overnight, for the all-clear siren, passing the time playing cards, talking or sleeping, while the war raged above them. Infants learned to sleep soundly during the din.

Songs and wry humor had the effect of calming young children. Adults would crack jokes about not being able to find their way around, as the topography topside was often radically altered when they emerged. There were tales about beds, sofas and commodes being hurled into trees, or blasted up to a neighbor's roof across the street. Children were cheerfully reminded to ask permission before shifting furniture. They certainly wouldn't want to be like the Germans, who lacked manners, would they? Mr. Longworth smiled. "We tykes were delighted, and we solemnly promised."

He told me about one fellow who found the top of his home gone. His wife commented that now he couldn't complain that the flat was too dark, since the Germans had given him a wonderful view, free. The man, not to be outdone, had noted that the breezes would "help me missus keep the dust down."

This incredible optimism was contagious, and it baffled the enemy. Surely what was happening in England shouldn't be cause for laughter! I think a sense of humor—and the optimism and grit it generated— was part of what won the war. (One bomb shelter's motto: *Keep London Tidy: Eat A Pigeon.*)

A London bus rider once told me his parents did a thriving business from their bombed-out front parlor, selling homegrown vegetables and "blast-treasure," like usable clothing, pot, pans, and, naturally, tins of salvaged tea. They earned just enough to buy groceries and a few little extras, like the rare chocolate bar for him.

He told me that everyone simply carried on with living, rarely look-ing back. "Me dad wouldn't allow sad thoughts. 'What's the good?' he'd say. 'We're alive. The rest is replaceable.' Going forward kept us busy and focused; we kids appreciated little things. Every day brought a new challenge. Everybody helped everybody. Nobody was fat, but nobody starved, either."

Such reflections leave me thoughtful for days.

A Feast of Words and Their Tweaks

Ending a sentence with a preposition is something up with which I will not put. —Winston Churchill

WORDS, FOR ME, ARE MORE delicious than chocolate sundaes, or midnight picnics on the beach. But when manhandled by verbal chiropractors, some words don't quite bear up under the strain.

Take, for example, A. Politicians and newsreaders portentously pronounce it aee instead of uh. They'd never say aee speaking extemporaneously, so its appearance on the scene is aee clear signal that something officiously pompous and stiff is about to emerge—usually while speak-reading from aee TelePrompTer. Today CNN announced: "Aee request for more calvary from top generals is being considered by brass." Oops. Later, channel-surfing, I heard that "Aeenother tornado has thumped Kansas hard." (These visual images rivet me.)

Contrary to popular belief, watching the Weather Channel is never dull. Once I heard a meteorologist mention Stradivarius clouds forecasted for my Sunday. And prepositions in that newsroom climb over one another like puppies. "This dangerous storm, moving on in from the Pacific Northwest, is racing on out over the plains on your Tuesday. It threatens insecure trailer parks; the National Weather Service advises moving on down into shelters, soon. There's multiple systems that could develop at any point in time as it moves through on up over the Midwest…" (Honest. I taped it.)

My Tuesday. Sigh. I suppose it's another American's Wednesday where the multiple systems is developing. I gave are and other plural verbs a New Orleans-style funeral years ago. Meteorologists' prepositional pileups pepper viewers. Perhaps they hope that presenting weather science that way will sound less intimidating, folksier, and, well, cooler. (Sorry; I couldn't resist.)

Such silliness is not confined to the Weather Channel, though. Recently a male anchor declared that House Speaker Nancy Pelosi had "thrown a wench in the works with her inflaming pre-vote speech." Heavens to Betsy!

With the TV mercifully silenced, I venture into the real world, only to overhear more stunners. "We saw a Spanish flamingo dancer." "I was so ravishingly hungry I gouged myself with food." "It was really his only idiotsyncrasy." "Pass the baslamic vinegar…" One elderly lady, trading ailments with a friend on the garden bench, declared that her bronical tubes and anal spinster had malfunctioned, requiring extensive medical treatment. Developing a huge coughing fit, I fled into the house to release the demon Laughter.

Why do we insert and when declaring the year, depending on which year it is? Two thousand and nine? We never say nineteen and ninety two. There is some mysterious agreement, never overtly stated, about and and year-recitations.

At this point in time is very popular now. Is this double emphasis meant to differentiate from a point in space? Why not say at this point, or at this time, or simply now? And everybody on TV who talks about the future takes care to specify that they are going forward. What other direction of time travel is there?! Moreover, how can something be very unique? There are no degrees of unique. Speaking of questions, let me ask you this. People routinely preface questions with Let me ask you this. Why not simply ask?

Healthy languages constantly evolve. Novel uses eventually find their way into dictionaries, becoming a permanent part of the lexicon. Sometimes perfectly good meanings are turned inside out. Thirty years ago, I lucked out meant I ran out of luck. Now it means I got lucky. Bad is now good. Hot is cool. The thing of it is is, there's some unfortunate evolutions. "I snuck into the house." "She's volumptuous." (Maintaining a straight face with that one can be very flustrating.)

Does anyone else notice this stuff, or are creative verbosity and grammatical tweaks just pigments of my overheated imagination?

That's a whole 'nother discussion.

The White Invader Sleighs England

ENGLISH UPPER LIPS HAVE WILTED significantly. A few inches of snow here, while fairly ho-hum to this Michigan resident, has undone Britain.

In my cottage deep in the countryside, three hours west of London, I have no TV; but the radio reports that trains, including the London underground, are at a standstill. Schools have closed, businesses have shut down, and roads are hopelessly clogged with millions of commuters trying to get home before more accumulation traps them in mid-London. People hike through London streets, begging for taxis, but drivers have abandoned their cabs and gone home on foot—or tried to. Buses aren't running. No one owns snow boots. Moving at all is a challenge. "This is definitely the worst snowstorm in seventy-five years," squawked the announcer. There are dire predictions of "worse to come." Good heavens! Such a lot of fuss over a few inches.

Things began innocently enough with snow sprinkles on Monday afternoon. By evening there was an inch of powder in my area, and the wind was blowing hard. Tuesday, all the airports gave up. One big jet skidded right off the runway. Ten inches is simply overwhelming here. And still, the snow falls.

Snug inside battered Bryn Garth Cottage, I feel right at home. Amid reports of school-free kids gleefully constructing snowmen and thumping cars with snowballs, I look out at a scene of incredible beauty. Our giant, centuries-old oaks are etched in white; the huge laurel hedge sags; wet snow makes curious changes in its posture. Through binoculars I observe shaggy-backed, white-powdered sheep baa-ing forlornly on steep hillsides; lambs peer around, uncertainly. Sheep are dim, but lambs are still inquisitive. This white stuff isn't uncomfortable, exactly, just odd. Between playful bounces they high-step, sniff the snow, and bleat. The old ladies complain, or graze as best they can.

As do I. The steep driveway leading to the highway is a sheet of ice. I'm trapped. So I've made do with three pieces of sliced ham, tea, and a half-loaf of stale bread. I snooze by the fire, waking to robins coaxing food from the wire feeders that line our porch. (I've witnessed English birds freeze to death on their branch-perches and topple to the ground. The few who've found my feeders may survive; oily seeds and nuts are great fuel.) Snuggling my hot-water bottle, I retreat to an icy bed with the radio still squawking about impassable roads. Accidents clog the few still open. The government has ground to a halt.

But think about it. England lies in the Gulf Stream, and parts of it are subtropical. Palm trees thrive in Cornwall. In such a country, snow brings chaos. People dare not step outside for fear of falling. (Many villagers frequent local shops every day or two for basic needs; now these shops are closed.) No one owns a snow shovel. ("What's that?" asked one man who was interviewed on the radio.) There's no salt to put down, no snowplows to manage icy, snow-packed roads. Slip-sliding cars on narrow lanes and carriageways alike bewilder seasoned

English drivers. Frantic commuters can't clear windscreens—no tools. It's nineteen degrees out there, not the more usual thirties or low forties, and folks caught away from home risk their pipes bursting—as our cottage's had.

But some things never change—or, rather, they always do. Buckingham Palace's Changing of the Guard looks ethereal, reports the news. Coal-black horses draped in red, carrying snowy guards with wilting, plumed hats, gingerly check to make sure they have firm ground under their hooves.

Yet thanks to our salt, snowplows, shovels, and savvy, in northern Michigan this weather wouldn't have merited so much as a school closing. Britain's panic isn't funny, but I smile, anyway. At least when it comes to snow, Americans are made of tough stuff.

Death's Nose Tweaked Twice

I WOKE TODAY, PADDED TO the dining room window and stared. Wow. Six more inches of snow had fallen during the night; there hasn't been this much in England in living memory. And it's still coming down. People's routines are paralyzed. Cars, buried in snow, are frozen into their spaces, and weak roofs are groaning under the weight. The elderly, who tend to shop daily for their simple needs, are trapped inside their homes. So they keep in touch with distressed relatives by telephone, drink tea to keep warm, and wait. Much of Europe is getting hammered, too.

Yesterday temperatures rose to just above freezing; the main roads cleared up a bit, allowing heavy traffic to move again on the busy A49 highway below our cottage.

A huge lorry from Cardiff arrived before noon to load up our drowned furniture to be dried and possibly repaired. But it couldn't make it up our long, steep driveway, though I'd shoveled all morning with a tiny coal shovel. (Remember, Brits have no winter tools of any kind—there is no need—so I used the only thing available.) I sprinkled the steepest parts of the driveway with every bit of table salt I had, and hoped for the best.

What happened was terrifying. Four times the huge truck, with its eight utterly inadequate summer-weight tires slid back eighty feet, nearly rolling into the busy two-lane highway. There was nothing for it but to tear off my bright red sweatshirt, run out into the highway, and flag down the whizzing traffic. This is incredibly dangerous; the curves in this road have taken many an unwary life. But the men in that lorry were frightened, and something had to be done. With much jumping and waving and running along the median, I stopped one lane, then the other. Once again, the furniture lorry backed/slid down, very carefully, well out into the road, with guidance from the helper. Then it got a looooong, running start (I yelled at him not to switch gears, but to remain in second—everyone here drives stick shifts) and roared up the driveway, the tires desperately clawing the icy tarmac. It just made it to the top—by a gnat's eyelash. For a second, I thought he'd slide back yet again and squish the guy directing him, but at least he wouldn't slide into oncoming traffic, and certain death.

With a big wave of thanks for the motorists I'd held at bay, I trundled up the long drive, grateful no one had been killed.

After they'd loaded up and downed many cups of sugared tea to soothe their shattered nerves, I stopped traffic again. The lorry, too enormous to turn around, backed, and slid, s-l-o-w-l-y down the long driveway into halted traffic, then roared safely off to Hereford, with a honk of thanks. I staggered into the cottage, desperate for another cuppa, and a nice treat—a teaspoon of whisky. After all, I'd shoveled mountains of snow with a teaspoon, and poked Death in the nose, twice. I deserved it.

Sketches of Alien Lives

WELL. HERE I SIT, toasting nicely in front of a cheerful kitchen fire. The wood snaps and hisses, radiating warmth in a snowy English world. The heating system soldiers on, thank goodness. After spoon-stout black coffee and bacon, I plan the day. Roofers won't show—it's snowing. Nobody owns a shovel, so people must cope with this bump in the season as best they can. Hmmm…I'll motor to Hereford for supplies, and ambiance.

It's always interesting. Along the High Street teen girls stroll by with exposed bellies and tight tops, sporting spiky purple and orange hair, often wearing unbuttoned, insubstantial coats. They seem impervious to the cold. Old people—late twenties and up—warmly bundled, trudge along, their gloved hands clutching shopping bags and parcels, ignoring them that can't be reasoned with.

Some shoppers have purchased cappuccinos and various sweets from outdoor vendors, and they sit outside under covered awnings, chatting and sipping, while big heaters glow red. It's odd, and charming.

Shop windows line the long, exceptionally wide, car-free street, trumpeting unprecedented price cuts—as much as seventy-five percent off merchandise consumers simply can't do without. Most are ignored.

The economy is shaky here; there's a feeling of unease and even fear just under the surface.

The thick, dirty glass of The Queen's Arms pub, a thousand years young, reveals beak-nosed old men sipping pints over lunch. Its famous, tattered ghost waits for more suitable conditions in which to drift around the premises. I've visited a few times, but the ghost manifests no interest in exposing itself to an inquisitive alien.

Sometimes, when I need cheering up, I'll trot to the old Green Dragon Hotel, smack in the middle of everything, to indulge in a cream tea before a lovely coal fire in the lounge. Long sofas and upholstered chairs, generous coffee tables and plump cushions greet me. What a change from stacked boxes and damp, dangling ceiling insulation! Warming an armchair, I order. Soon, hot scones topped with clotted cream and jam vanish, with tea in hot pursuit. I peck away at my laptop.

Suddenly, a woman with six young children enters, and heads confidently for an adjacent sofa. The little ones climb up onto its cushions, so small their dozen legs extend straight out. Their familiarity with this room is obvious. No menu card is necessary; the woman sits opposite, placing her order to a smiling waitress in a low murmur, while her brood sits quietly, whispering and giggling. She then goes around loosening hat strings and removing coats, making cheery comments. There is a feeling of ritual, of a cherished, special time reserved just for them. I see unmistakable evidence that these children are hers. Two are clearly twins. She is stocky, relaxed, and relates with them as a mother might. Each child is asked to share the most interesting thing he or she saw or did since the last visit; their accounts are delightful. British children have a wonderfully precise, melodic way of speaking that never fails to enchant me.

Finger-painting pictures while getting thumped on the head dominate the conversation. James had whacked Ian, but only with a rolled newspaper; general laughter greets this revelation. A four-year old smugly announces she had two helpings of strawberry ice cream yesterday. That was because Uncle Neville didn't want his, and the dog was outside.

Tea comes. Each mug hosts pot-warmed milk, a spoonful of sugar and a liberal splash of hot tea. Cookies are passed around. Everyone carefully sips and munches; giggles ring out when silly observations are traded.

I leave, more refreshed by this tableau than my solitary tea break could ever offer.

Soggy, Delicious Memories

I'M SITTING ON THE STRIPPED and unlovely floor of our flooded-out cottage in England, sifting through parental mementos. Here are limp old London Times Sunday magazines, kept for their wonderful commentaries, or for the alphabetical listing of the one thousand most influential people of the twentieth century, or for anything that caught my mother's eye.

Hmmm. Here's something on tail-less cats.

My mother had the gift of curiosity. She loved to read about simply everything—the universe's origins, biographies of politicians, why tigers have stripes. A great experimenter, she read cookbooks gleefully. Some of the results wanted a decent burial; most were wonderful.

Occasionally, I rediscover treasures. A clammy page, pried apart, reveals a cherished poem about a tree at the end of its life. Mother loved trees; one photograph shows David and her standing next to an immense seven-hundred-year-old oak that gave shade during England's Great Plague and still lives happily outside a nearby country pub, the Lough Pool.

Memories surface. I recall sitting inside an even bigger, older, thriving tree in a Gloucester churchyard. Its massive lower branches now rest quietly on the ground, too long and heavy to remain suspended. The earth, over the centuries, has gently risen to meet them; I could tell the tree appreciated the support. In spite of that hollow heart, Tree was fully dressed in green that day, soaking up the sun, utterly content. The churchyard's ancient, teetering tombstones keep it company.

And what's this? A flat, tissue-wrapped stone bears the fossil of a hundred-million-year-old tubeworm she'd carried for a quarter-century in her jeans pocket, after spotting it one day on a cold Scottish beach. She'd fingered it so many times that it was polished.

My mother died amazed that death was happening: she had so much to do, to see, to taste, to learn, and suddenly, she blinked out. A poem she loved—with just seven lines—reads:

A Life

Innocence?
In a sense—
In NO sense.

WAS that it?
Was THAT it?
Was that IT?

That was it.

Oh! Here's a magazine's picture of a gorgeous, fully-dressed, delectable hamburger. In a margin she'd written "Frame this!" Heavens— I know why!

One summer lunchtime, Mom was at a craft show in the little Welsh town of Abergavenny where she was selling her beautiful handcrafted clocks (the royal entourage actually bought one once). She formed a plump, three-quarter-pound hamburger paddy from butcher-bought ground (the British say "minced") beef, to cook on a nearby communal grill.

On a plate she laid out slices of onion, Double Gloucester cheese, and a respectable hunk of crisp lettuce alongside a generous bun. Ketchup and English mustard stood guard. A small gathering watched, fascinated. One amused Welshman couldn't resist a comment: "M'love, tha' overweight meat pile canno' stick together withou' cereal and additives." (British burgers are kept together with such filler.)

Mom looked up, astonished, then grinned. "Why ever not?"

People stared, then settled back to watch ruin happen. This silly, deluded American didn't have a clue.

She popped the naked burger on the grill, adding seasoned salt and freshly ground pepper. It sizzled happily. A quick flip to cook the other side to medium-rare, and she slid it onto the toasted bun, added the condiments, and downed it triumphantly, chasing it with a chilled, local beer. Quiet reigned.

Suddenly, latecomers edged forward, proffering bills, saying, "Eh! I'll have one o' those!" The bewildered grillmaster stood, open-mouthed, amid the clamor of futile, shouted orders. Licking her fingers, Mom reclaimed her spatula, thanked him, and strode off replete, and delighted.

Americans may be brash, she gloated to herself, and wet behind the ears. But by golly, we know hamburgers!

Oops! Bonked-Brain Bloopers

Bemuse

SIX YEARS AGO MY BRAIN'S circuitry got muddled after a near-fatal auto accident. For a while there, I didn't know what from whom. Rebooting has been a fascinating challenge.

Front-garden encounters demonstrate my difficulties. "Hi, Dee!" Cheerful greetings sail toward me from people whose faces I must have known once. But I haven't a clue who they are until they remind me that, say, they live next door. Curiously, folks named after flowers, like Violet or Rose, are easier to recall.

I've had to completely relearn my garden, starting with the vocabulary. For example, I'd reason that lilies and daylilies were the same. The name lily was simply a shortened form of daylily—right? But, of course, they're very different plants. For a good while I'd pronounce Canna lilies as canonized, garnering more than one odd look. (Their fancy red flower hats and imposing purple bodies suggested cardinals, the kind that live in Rome but can't fly, and that led to thoughts of saints, and saints are canonized...)

Early in the untangling process, I interpreted words like relish literally. Relish was food. Just food. Now, as I mend, I relish its versatility, and make sentences tastier by saucily tossing relish in…Ha! Or I'd brush my hairs. Hair was one hair, for heaven's sake. Why bother to brush just one? Obviously, I had millions. Now that's sorted.

After the accident, I couldn't be down in the dumps. That expression baffled me. Clearly, I lived in town, and dumps are in remote locations, in high, smelly piles—not my sort of place. Besides, it's impossible to be in more than one dump at a time, anyway.

Sometimes, searching for the usual words, I come up with new ones. Some seem much more reasonable. I sometimes "attach strings to formal holes" (plug cords into outlets). Nail clippers have become snappers. Cars' hoods are snouts. Sticks are stalks.

I have a problem humping M's. Any word with more than one m in a row, like "communication," throws me. Once I begin writing them, my pen insists on continuing their humps…Mmmmmm. But it isn't just handwriting. Oddly, even typing double-M words also requires tongue-biting concentration.

Even more confusing than words are number games, which trip my circuitry. To make sense to me, numbers need to be assigned to things, like bank accounts or addresses or bills. Deliberate mix-ups in, say, Sudoku make no sense, so I look away, confused and unraveled. Numbers in piles have no meaning, and so there.

These problems persist today. Recently, I wrote about the mashed potato man, and credited Tchaikovsky with The Lone Ranger's theme. Wrong! It came from Rossini's *William Tell Overture*. But the Russian got the credit, because I'd heard his overture first. (Even though my little voice did ding an alarm, it can be irritatingly unhelpful about exactly how I'm wrong.)

As my brain doc put it, "Your circuitry is down, but not out. Reason-able reassembly will happen, with time."

When first planting bulbs, nearly eighteen years ago, I had no clue which end was up. Bulbs don't always have points, or roots dangling out the bottom to make the decision easy. They just rest there in the palm of one's hand, innocently hopeful that the gardener will get it right. But, far from being dim bulbs, they know what's what. Though I planted them upside down, all eventually turned up. Literally.

Sure enough, like the bulbs, my convoluted words and thoughts have gradually righted themselves.

I look ahead to my next blooper with curiosity. Mostly, columns just fall out of me, but as I cheerfully romp through the alphabet's twenty-six zillion combinations, I commit inevitable alphabetical sins. So they're written decently in advance, then allowed to simmer; silly word choices become obvious the next morning, when I'm fresh.

Spotting my odd spellings, and clarifying perceptions teaches patience, which, like the nursery rhyme, is a virtue…and virtue is a Grace…who is, apparently, a little girl with a dirty face—but why?

Now I know the answer. Sort of…

British English Baffles Bumpkin

A COMMON LANGUAGE SEPARATES Brits and Yanks. Recently, shopping for a new stove in an English superstore, I inquired where they might be found. After some curious looks ("It's too cold to camp, surely?") people directed me to an outdoor area, which offered "wee" prima stoves. Mystified by the miscommunication, I waved my arms to indicate size. "Och—you're needing a hob!" Er, yeah, that.

A faucet was next. But this word was also met with rapid, nervous blinks. "Eh, we don't do that…" said the baffled clerk. Finally, I dragged the guy over to one, and pointed. Enlightened, he smiled. "Ah… a tap!"

American clapboard houses intrigue the workmen; everyone here has brick or stone homes. One fellow bashing down our flood-wreaked kitchen cabinets joked that he knew how the name happened: "Americans just clap therr bloody boards on and fasten 'em down, eh? They's no' as sturdy, surely? Yer hurricanes would no' bother a proper stone cottage, I'll wager…"

Black Pudding (pig's blood, globules of fat, and raisins), Spotted Dick (a sort of spongy cake with raisins), and Toad-in-a-Hole (sausages in batter) are popular restaurant selections here. Wouldn't you be riveted by such names, and keen to inspect what the servers plunked down?

I gape at some of the more popular supermarket offerings, including barbecued pigs' trotters and slow-roasted, spicy pork bellies, but I haven't tried those yet. There are limits. (Wait! Aren't pork bellies a stock market thing?)

When I mentioned longing for a hamburger, the same workman grinned. "There in't no ham in them things, so why mention the piggies? Yanks be city folk; they don' grasp the difference, surely?" The other men exploded into laughter. "Aye, but pigs an' cows booth have hamstrings, so tha' is where the confusion lies, surely?" Huge guffaws all around.

And what, pray, are digestive biscuits? Are all the others INdigestible? This bumpkin is regularly flummoxed.

Yesterday I was offered a portion of lamb's liver sandwich swathed in English mustard, served with a slab of Leicester (say "Lester") cheese and a plump pickle. Hmmm. Actually, it wasn't too bad.

But crusty bread is dying. I popped down to Wormelow Tump's shop to taste their freshly baked bread, but sadly, it's gone soft. My inquiries regarding firm exteriors earned blank stares.

I love bread that stays stiff when I whack it; a firm crust should cuddle a delicious, yeasty interior. Proper stiff-upper-lip bread can be tossed, like a football, and caught, un-dented. But no. Today a loaf loafs; its wafer-thin crust collapses when touched by shoppers. Ugh. Five limp loaves were rejected, as they drooped miserably when held. I've resigned myself instead to long stiff French loaves that my teeth are pleased to tackle. But French bread? In England? Sigh...The workmen commented that they didn't like to "work" tough crusts. Ah, well.

I prowl grocery aisles for cans, er, tins—of beef and noodles, eaten cold, as our hob's been chucked out.

Fresh fruit, a cooked supermarket chicken and a scrumptious Guinness beer cake (baked by a sympathetic Wormelow resident who knows my plight) keep me going nicely. Meanwhile, the workmen and I chat as we work, and linguistic gems fall into my lap. "Tha's a dog's dinner" (fine kettle of fish). "Me wife's gone flat" (She's feeling down). "I'm stretching me braces" (suspenders—I'm getting fat). "Gitaway!" (You don't say!). "I'm corked up" (constipated). "Take the dual carriageway" (highway).

At intervals we "park our trotters," and enjoy "a wee strupak" (a Scots workman's description of tea and crumpets) with HobNob cookies. (Its motto: "One nibble and you're nobbled!")

Here's to many more outrageous British/American exchanges. Clink!

Missing Thoughts, and Miss Charlotte

LATELY, WELL INTO THE RESTORATION of flood-ruined Bryn Garth Cottage, I'll jolt awake, startled to find myself still in England. Climbing out of my warm nest, I begin the day with crisp bacon, strong black (canned) coffee, and a vague heartache.

I miss the sniffs of home. There's a special scent—okay, an odor—associated with one's own nest. I miss that.

I long for my airy, clean kitchen, the perky sound of boiling water added to freshly ground coffee beans that vanquish mental cobwebs. I miss cooking—anything.

I miss clean windows. I have bare walls here—bare, stud-exposed walls.

I miss people. In Traverse City I can pop outside to shovel snow, and passers-by toss cheery greetings my way. I miss the mail carrier, who always delivers a smile, and the laughter of my neighbor's children. I miss trotting down to Burritt's Market and chatting with Joel, who mans the meat counter, or hallooing the nice ladies at Potter's Bakery as I join the other drooling sugar-junkies in line for our fixes.

There are foxes here, and voles, and an incredible variety of birds visiting my feeders in Helen's Wood, our forest. There are vast carpets of snowdrops, bluebells, daffodils, tulips, primroses, and wild rhododendrons. Fresh lambs bounce about on the distant hillsides. The Welsh Black Mountains are lovely behind the little village of Wormelow Tump, where cottage chimneys emit thin plumes of straight-up smoke. Rabbits box on the lawn, and nibble new blades of grass flavored by tiny English daisies. There is lots of life up here, but none of it speaks English.

I don't miss the TV's incessant silliness, the opinion-laden news, the ridiculous ads, the noise. I don't miss the thump-boom of unattached males' car radios as they drive the city's streets, announcing their availability. I don't miss the sound of ambulance sirens telegraphing someone's distress as they rush to Munson Hospital.

Here it is silent, except for the world turning, and the animals responding to nature's rhythm. The stars are shockingly vivid.

Yesterday I found a tiny frog, who sat timidly in the palm of my hand, his back moist and twiggy. Flakes of rich, green moss decorated his delicate head.

A large, furtive rat scurries across the lawn into the thick laurel. (At least he dashed away from the cottage.)

I rake; the sound mingles with the raucous screams of crows, and the forlorn sound of English mourning doves, whose coos are longer, and more complicated.

I was pulling on a sweater one morning last week in our large master bath, when suddenly my neck hairs twitched. I was being observed. Hmmm. You know the feeling.

Sure enough, when I slowly turned around, there sat a black spider watching me from the porcelain acreage of the tub's edge. She was utterly still, jet-black, huge—more than three inches of arachnid beauty—and didn't mind being noticed. I pulled the stool closer, and we examined each other. She showed no fear, only curiosity. Each slim—er, foot—grasped the sleek white rim confidently. Those enormous eyes looked: I looked. Aliens, both of us—I with my horrid, misshapen, practically limbless body, and my rear end without spinnerets. I was probably pitied.

On the other hand, I admired Miss Charlotte. She was leggy, agile, beautiful, well fed, and perhaps a mite over-confident about showing herself, hmmm?

We came to an agreement. She'd stay out of my shoes and clothes, and I'd stay out of her tub and use only the shower, which is in its own stall. We were together for weeks, and I confess it was nice to go into the bathroom and know she'd be in there. A friend with eight legs is better than none at all.

Storm Over Aberystwyth

MY CHEERFUL YOUNGER DAUGHTER LISA whisked me off to a Welsh coastal college town, Aberystwyth, for a two-day holiday. She knew it well, having visited it once on spring break from college in London.

The three-hour trip was a jaw-dropper. Our little car clawed its way up mountains into clouds delivering misty rain. My eyes were on stalks; my hands strangled the wheel as I drove on the British side of the narrow road chanting, "Keep left; don't *look* left..."

But, Oh! When I occasionally dared a glance, holes in the fog revealed sheer cliffs, rich greenery, bored sheep—and nobody. We were on top of the Welsh world, alone. Occasionally, giant boulders, teetering high above us, contemplated whether to be merciful, or murderous. The wire netting that surrounded them looked pathetically inadequate. I was not confident.

Finally, Aberystwyth emerged, curling like a collar around Cardigan Bay. Our delightful room boasted floor-to-ceiling windows that overlooked the heaving ocean bashing away at the promenade below. (One is never more than seventy-five miles from the sea anywhere in Britain.)

Craving exercise, we decided to climb a monstrous 450-foot high lump of black rock at the edge of the sea. Dominating the town, it's known as Constitution Hill. The wind was tolerant, teasing my hat at every turn on the steep path, without actually snatching it. Pausing to catch my breath before entering the cliff-top café, I beheld a stunning aspect. The sea's infinitely long, frothy tongue lapped the pebbled beach far below; a mile-long connected curve of little hotels, shops and university buildings lined the beachfront, finished by a ruined castle. Two rubber-clad surfers who'd dared the waves on this blustery midday waded hastily out of the pounding surf. An immense, roiling black cloud, pregnant with rain, was rushing toward the little town.

Snug inside the warm, glass-lined restaurant, which was curiously round in shape, my daughter and I sipped coffee and tasty bowls of tomato-basil soup while nervously watching the storm roar toward us. The room trembled. I felt suddenly insignificant, and far too vulnerable, perched precariously atop this immense rock.

Blackness enveloped the sturdy structure, which shook but held. Outside, a heavy wooden picnic table blew over. A grinning metal alligator, with a child-sized hole in its head for parental pictures, shrieked, then split in half. We gasped and stared, helpless and afraid. Five minutes later, bouncing hailstones, lashing, icy rain, and fifty-mile-an-hour winds had passed us, heading straight for the tender new lambs that fed on the green hills, inland.

Suddenly the sun emerged, illuminating Cardigan Bay so intensely it was impossible to look at it.

We'd survived. Everything for miles had been scoured clean. Long rows of close-built stone cottages gleamed; their tiled roofs, looking for all the world like crisp stitches on a vast green quilt, shone wetly on the hills above the town.

The girls manning the lunch counter tittered nervously; speaking Welsh, they pointed at the upturned outdoor furniture. This had been an unusually violent squall.

After lunch we wisely rode the Victorian mountain tram down, to avoid being blown away. The wind that always follows frontal systems roared; holding tight to each other, we staggered thankfully into the little open car. Gorse bushes, brandishing long needle-spikes and bright yellow flowers, squatted menacingly along the rocky path, waiting to stab foolish hikers. Our jerky descent was nearly straight down, noisy, and fun.

We sought our lovely room, shivering, awed and bone-tired. What an introduction to Aberystwyth's wilder side!

TV Thump-Thump Woes—and Excesses

IF I HAD THE POWER, I'd change how TV works.

I'd start with the news. One person would read the news. Not two, which is an excess of bodies for a paucity of information. Once, I was behind the scenes in a television studio, and saw for myself how spoon-fed it all is. Reader One begins reading the TelePrompTer, then a partner carries on once differently-colored letters scroll by. Often the first reader manages only two sentences before Reader Two is scripted to interrupt.

I miss Walter Cronkite's simple desk. Those have mostly vanished, to be replaced by stage sets, enormous, blindingly colorful and ever-changing, in the ceaseless competition for viewers. One hyped-up anchor, clutching notes, dashes from a vast "reporting" area to another huge room crammed with floor-to-ceiling monitors, each dangling a different story. All that running around introduces a note of hysteria. The anchor's voice rises; his voluminous verbal diarrhea overwhelms viewers. I'd eliminate this guy's caffeine intake, and suggest meditation.

Everyone looks uncomfortably on display. The lovely anchorwomen wear low-cut blouses and skimpy skirts. They must stand, teetering on spiky heels; perch on stools; or manage large sofas in vast, multi-colored arenas, surreptitiously tugging at their clothing. Less reveal-ing clothes? Not allowed. (Ratings.)

When was the last time you heard news without adornment? Doesn't happen. Muzak-scream, frantic drum-bumps, and outrageous visual shenanigans make the words spoken by newsreaders, or ad announc-ers, practically impossible to discern. Billy Mays screams his product's charms. Shepard Smith must compete with incredible background booms during his "Around the World in Eighty Seconds." Why must it be so loud? Perhaps aging producers once worked with rock bands; their ears, damaged by high-decibel sounds, must not hear what's happening. And every few seconds there are loud whizzing sounds as some new logo zips next to, or underneath, the main frame. Pop-ups of teeny people, making absurd gestures, distract, rather than attract. Wired producers must be exhausted, trying to think up new ways of pouncing on ears and eyes. *I'm* exhausted, as I wade through the noise toward the rarity of clar-ity. But I honestly don't think narrators could function if the accompa-nying background rhythm-bump vanished. They'd feel naked and lost.

Most news doesn't deserve the name. Three percent of the hour offers factual information; the rest is opinion, gossip and speculation. With TV running 24/7, rubbish rules. I'd offer news just three times a day, with news flashes as needed, and give everyone a break.

I understand that ads are necessary to pay for the programs. But they're so intrusive—ads during dramas begin seamlessly, with no pause from storylines—and there are so many of them. Ten long, bor-ing "messages" precede each bit of story. I've counted. And these run over and over. An actor says a product's name three times, or three different actors say the name; I feel hammered.

Grammatical errors make many advertisements absurd, but no one cares. One guy begins his sales pitch by asking, "Are you limited by your mobility?" Er, what? Two years later, that sentence hasn't changed. The product, a nifty motorized chair, seems useful, but the fellow touting it needs to reconsider his phrasing. Speaking of absurd, how desperate must actors be to dress as grapes, electricity, or a pepperoni pizza?

Whether on news programs, ads, or fictional dramas, viewers are directed how to feel. A deep, sustained bass fiddle note is supposed to summon sadness or apprehension, while super-rapid bangs and clatters mean murder and mayhem. Naturally, orchestral violins indicate mush is afoot. When every plot twist seems to require a new musical genre, I feel patronized.

And whatever happened to discretion? Kissing is open-mouthed; one actor lunches on the other. And like the news anchors, all CSI female stars—even the "coroners"—are, er, hanging out.

Are viewers so jaded that these assaults are necessary to hold our interest? I dunno. But my mute button is worn out. Catching up on substantive news is difficult now. I get thump-jumpy, and abandon ship. Enough is enough. During laundry-folding time I hunt for a program like "The Twilight Zone." The relative quiet is shocking.

Better yet, I'll indulge in a crisp apple and a good book, punctuated by the sound of silence. Bliss.

Kate: How She Saved Her Own Life

GASPING, I TIGHTENED MY FACE mask, trying to cope with billowing dust and floating fiberglass remnants. Workmen restoring our flooded-out cottage in England were lining the walls and ceilings with insulation before applying plasterboard. Rearranging some dusty papers, I noticed a grimy photo of Mom and David's slim, lovely Alsatian dog, Kate. Her head rested on his knee; her eyes were locked on his, full of love. She'd died in his arms four years ago, of extreme old age. The picture triggered a glowing memory of her first day with them.

In 1989, a year after their beloved elderly lab Fred died, Mother and David decided to adopt another dog. Off they trooped to the Hereford city pound to inspect the hopeful residents. An exhausted young Alsatian with enormous stand-up ears bearing scab-crusted tips shot them a despairing look. (Mom's cherished childhood "police" dog, Alex, wore that same terrible look when her family left him behind when moving in 1930. It still haunted her.)

This dog's history was unnerving. She'd been dumped on the road, filthy, frightened, and ear-injured; someone had tortured her. Less than two years old, she was soon adopted by a family, but was quickly returned when they'd found her aggressive behavior alarming.

As it happens, David has an almost magical way with dogs. Animals adore him. After talking with the staff, they decided to take her on trial; it was her last chance.

The beautiful, frightened dog was walked to the car; as she was put in back, she snapped at David. Instantly he looked her straight in the eye, and roared "No!" Shocked, the dog sat, miserable. David held onto the moment, before finally releasing her from The Look. Speaking gently, he reassured her with a few soft words. The ride home was silent.

She was taken quietly out of the car on a lead, ushered into the cottage and shown water and a bowl of dry food, which she ignored. Off the lead now, she explored her surroundings, her hackles rising as cat was scented. (Jinjii had removed herself from view, but was watching this shocking turn of events with her usual feline equanimity.)

Mother and David sat at the dining room table, talking quietly to her. Kate stopped and looked at her new owners; her tail twitched tentatively. But she kept her distance. Suddenly, David coughed. Cringing, the nervous animal urinated on the carpet, just a little bit.

Now came the miracle. Kate was absolutely horrified by this breach. With a low whimper she sneaked a look at David, hoping he hadn't noticed. Then she furtively pawed a small area rug lying nearby, maneuvering it carefully over the "mistake." Finally, she sat on it, head down, huge ears flat against her head. She dared to look up. Mother and David stared back, open-mouthed, disbelieving.

She was in.

David put Jinjii-cat on Mom's lap and introduced the two animals. Kate snarled and lunged. David, talking quietly, held the leash taut, and amazingly, Jinjii kept her claws sheathed, content to trust her people to keep things reasonable. Inch by inch Kate was allowed closer; Jinjii, eyes closed, tolerated the huge dog's terrifying advance. Their noses touched. Fascinated, Kate deep-sniffed every single inch of Jinjii's fur. The cat purred. Kate's tail wagged. David released her.

And that was that.

For nearly a decade the two animals shared house and grounds, and even napped together, with Jinjii snug next to Kate's belly. Not once did they fight.

Kate knew she was a lucky dog. Like Jinjii, she'd found her heaven.

A Mothering Sunday Rescue

THE BRITISH CELEBRATED MOTHERING SUNDAY on a sunny, warmish March 22. I spent that afternoon wandering Hereford's ancient, tree-lined park, content to observe parents enjoying the profuse flowers with their children on this special day. "Today's about praising mothers," solemnly intoned one little guy wearing knee socks, short gray pants, a little coat, tie and hat. (He reminded me of John-John Kennedy, saluting his presidential father.) Mums knew that today somebody else would prepare the Sunday roast. Dads smiled, and even family pets seemed delighted as they strained at their leashes.

Huge, century-old, leaf-bare oaks lined the paths. The River Wye tumbled vigorously along; rubber-clad fishermen standing in waist-deep water cast their lines, filling floating baskets with flapping fish. There were cheers from the appreciative audience that watched from the white Victorian footbridge, which was suspended over the river and looked for all the world like a miniature Brooklyn Bridge. Large, colorful primrose-stuffed flowerbeds shouted spring. Food vendors strategically clustered around the graceful bridge sold cappuccinos, candy, and, of course, wonderful Cornish ice cream, a perennial favorite with everyone.

I noticed one woman with a boy, perhaps eight, in tow; his eyes lit up when they came upon the vendor selling "ices." "Please, Mum, can I have one?" She smiled, and said, "Why not?" He made his selection, and indulged contentedly on a sunny bench along the flower-lined path.

Something about the woman's demeanor seemed—off. Her smile was ready, but reserved. She looked sad. In one hand the boy clutched a helicopter, making zooming noises between licks. Mum looked away. Hmmm. I decided her husband might be in Iraq. Hereford is home to a squadron of the secretive, exclusive Special Air Service (SAS), which is perhaps best known for its successful rescue of hostages during the 1980 siege at the Iranian Embassy in London. That feat won the SAS much unwanted publicity.

As he sat beside her, legs dangling, the child looked thoughtfully across the path toward the bedding plants. It was easy to read his mind. I imagined his dad saying "Watch over your mum while I'm away, son." This was her special day, and he wanted to mark it—but how? Proper English lads would never pick bedding flowers—but what about the ones growing with cheerful abandon in the short grass? There were fat dandelions, and lots of bright English daisies, and even a lovely reddish pinecone, just there, along the path.

He studied the situation for as long as it took to finish the ice cream, but just before biting into the cone he turned, suddenly. "Mum, will you do something for me?" Puzzled, but game, she smiled. "Right, James—what is it?"

"Don't look for a minute, please," he said, with a smile. She obligingly closed her eyes. He ran to the rain-dampened earth beside the river fence, and, scooping up a handful of soil, stuffed it into the soggy cone. The little pinecone went in next. (A smile told me a pine-coned ice cream cone appealed to his sense of fun.) Finally, he plucked the nearest two long-stemmed dandelions, then snatched a cluster of tiny daisies, stuffing both artlessly into his clever container. Marching to his mother, arm flung out, he offered his masterpiece, saying, "Ta-da! You can look, now!"

She did, and her laughter rang across the green. Her cheeks brightened as she took the arrangement, exclaiming with genuine delight. It was clever; he knew it. As they rose to leave, she stood straighter, her step was firm, and James looked at her, knowing he'd made a difference. His helicopter happily "flew" around his mother, and she grinned.

That ice-cream-cone-bouquet had definitely rescued—and sweetened—her day.

Bangs, Bruises, and Blink-Outs

TICK-TOCK. TIME DASHES ON, and my flooded-out cottage renovation in England is progressing. Shortly, I'll be gone. Every minute counts. Nobody in England worked for four days at Easter—more time lost. The cottage must be finished by April's end. It will be a near thing.

But there are setbacks. Some hurt. Running confidently along the path to the front door, I forgot to remember a substantial stair level change. Stepping into thin air, I fell head-over-teakettle, landing in an undignified sprawl on a lower stone landing. My tumble must have been spectacular; workmen came rushing up to see what was left. Bruised and embarrassed, I checked for limb-wobble—nothing amiss, thank goodness—gathered the shreds of my dignity and carried on, scraped and dented, like the car (from miscalculating absurdly teeny British parking spaces). The painter, distracted by my fall, spilled a gallon of emulsion on the driveway; the electrician pulled an arm muscle jumping off his ladder to help, and one carpenter, seeing that I'd live, waved his saw and joked, "You'll no' be needin' my services, then, eh?"

Plaster and stone dust-coated boxes crammed with various goods, utensils, et cetera are piled everywhere. I still have no heat, and only one hard-working plug. Finding my worker-shifted toaster is always interesting; today it's parked under the dining table in the sunroom, and has to be tipped over and shaken to eliminate plaster bits. The poor coffeepot gasps and puffs, nearly overwhelmed. There is absolutely nothing I can do about it. Dusty thou art, and dusty thou shalt remain, for probably one more week.

Today the vital washing machine coughed and died with a squawk; I immediately ordered an inexpensive, reconditioned one. The eager merchant promised delivery and installation in just an hour; plus, he'd haul away the dead one, if I'd have a check ready. Done.

I look like a chocolate-smeared, powdered doughnut; covered in plaster dust, I sport an oak-stained nose and hands from wiping ceiling beams. I keep teams of men—electricians, carpenters, plumbers, painters, gas men—supplied with tea and sweets, and help out where I can.

Today, applying brown stain to the exterior garage wall, I looked up to see a beautiful red fox sitting on a clump of snowdrops, watching me curiously, from perhaps fifteen feet away. (Bryn Garth Cottage backs up to a forest, Helen's Wood, where hunting is forbidden, so its inhabitants aren't as wary.) Then, suddenly ignoring me, he stared intently down his pointed nose into the foliage. A few motionless seconds later he pounced on something three feet away from his forepaws. A mouse, lost in thought, lost his life. He ate it head-first, in a few gulps; the wee tail flicked for a second, like a last wave, from the side of Reynard's mouth. Then, shooting me a glance, he yawned and disappeared over a rise, before I could grasp what had happened. There was just the faintest rustling, then, a blink later, no fox...

Helen's Wood is a photographer's dream. Hundreds of thousands of colorful wildflowers blanket its leaf-rich ground and steep hills. The narrow, winding path beckoned. Enchanted, and needing to dim the death of the mouse, I put down my brush and succumbed to the magic. Limping awkwardly along in dappled sunlight through perfumed air, amid ancient, budding trees and nesting birds, I mused that the mouse was probably young, and definitely foolish. (Do wild mice ever get old?) But then, aging doesn't matter that much, unless you are a cheese. It's how well you live, not how long, isn't it?

Ancient Chester — Moans and Marvels

ON APRIL 9 MY HUSBAND rolled into Hereford on the noon train. He'd gotten the "wrinklie rate," a five-day four-hundred-dollar round-trip ticket from Detroit to London. His office was closed for Easter, anyway, and it was his birthday. After he'd cheered my flooded-out cottage renovations, we motored to Chester. It's a town not quite three hours away that lies along the tidal River Dee, just two miles from the Welsh border,.

This ancient city of about eighty thousand souls is a World Heritage site. Over two thousand years ago, busy Romans built pillared gardens, huge arches, and a eight-thousand-seat amphitheatre there, all of which are now partially excavated. Multiple medieval black-and-white timbered buildings sprang up later; restored, they're still stunning. Its ancient cathedral, with an intriguing mixture of styles, is the third most visited in Britain. But the two-mile-long brick-and-stone Roman wall that nearly surrounds Chester is my favorite marvel.

Our arrival was marred by disappointment. I'd found an attractive-looking B & B online; it had a nice write-up and was located a short walk from the center of town, but the reality was shocking. To be frank, the picture lied. Cement covered everything, including the patio and "garden." No grass anywhere. A spindly, fifteen-story-high derrick dangled directly overhead. The walled parking area was girdle-tight; I had to get out and guide Joe as he edged the car along inch by inch. Bulging trash bags lined the garden wall's edges—another bad sign. We found the hidden key in the old outhouse, and climbed nervously up to our room. Horrors!

This bilious boudoir had two badly made beds crammed into an extremely narrow space. Joe quick-peeked at the bedsheets, flea-hunting. (We'd gotten a big dose, years ago, when I'd found us an awful room in Rome. I seem to have mastered the art of booking badly.) The bathroom was the size of a cancelled postage stamp. A desperately sad window looked out on—more cement. This long-dead room wanted a decent burial. We shuddered. A look was exchanged. After stampeding out, I stopped traffic, he hastily backed out, I leaped in, and we were gone, fists punching air, shouting with relief.

Six blocks away we found The Pied Bull Pub/Inn, Chester's oldest coachhouse, which dated from 1144 and was situated right in the middle of town. Two minutes later we'd secured its last enormous room, boasting a lovely four-poster bed, sofa, matching chairs, coffee table, armoire, generous bath, glorious window, breakfast. It was cheap as dirt in the off-season. I never wanted to leave!

According to the literature in our room, two ghosts haunt the place. I questioned the withered front-desk lady. "Yes, indeed," she said, "I've seen the ruffled gentleman three times over the years, but, so far, not the parlor maid. Muriel has, though…" Looking thoughtful, she stared into space for a bit. "He never speaks, just looks out yon window…He's no trouble."

The fish and chips supper was yummy, but breakfast was awful: instant coffee was served! The next morning we found a little shop a block away, with lace tablecloths and lovely cups, and savored the brewed beans. Ahhh! A full English breakfast, with unbuttered toast-in-a-rack-so it can-get-cold-quicker, were cheerfully downed.

Here's an interesting fact: In Britain, if you order coffee, you'll get one cup. Might be instant. Might not. (Ask, if you care.) Some bigger hotel chains set a steaming carafe before you, but most ordinary eateries offer ONE pour. So I order "Americano" (which is presented in a giant-sized cup), and make it last. I love England, but this is a moan for me.

Fortified, we circumnavigated the Roman wall and peered down at the splendid, grandstanded racecourse and the gaily-painted houseboats that navigated the River Dee's hand-cranked locks. The panoramic Turner landscape was flooded with light.

Eventually we left the wall to wander the ancient cobbled streets downtown, which were lined with stunning, completely restored black-and-white buildings. One could imagine Romans clattering along these generous avenues in their chariots. We bought another coffee, split a roll, and marveled at the architecture surrounding us.

Chester is a good-sized city, its curving streets full of modern mini-malls set inside these ancient structures. It's cleverly done, causing no offense to a critical eye. Some buildings housed small shops crammed full of merchandise, mostly tourist-oriented. Some offered second-floor access, where people and pigeons could sit in open balconies and look down at the long, wide thoroughfares. Cars were not permitted downtown, so families milled around on foot, peeking into centuries-old windows at elegant clothing, shoes, or local artists' pottery or paintings. The stained-glass cathedral was newer, but still very old by American standards. It looked well-settled there, framed by a fence and a grassy expanse. Its well-tended flowerbeds brightened the gloomy stone facade.

A town crier shouted news to delighted explorers and happy shoppers. Scenes like this guarantee many happy returns!

Two Disasters That Didn't Happen

As I applied a rich mahogany stain to the porch stairs of our flood-renovated cottage in England, a workman scraping ivy-covered walls nearby suddenly asked, "What was the stupidest thing you've ever done—and gotten away with?"

Oh, boy. What a fascinating question. Doing boring, repetitive stuff, like scraping and staining, gives birth to interesting conversation.

I stared at the guy, nibbled my lip, then grinned. That one was easy.

"Well, one summer day about twenty-five years ago, I decided to clean the master bedroom in our newly remodeled home…"

I'd dusted, vacuumed, and generally alarmed a lot of dust bunnies. Then, inspired, I decided to change our king-sized waterbed's water. It had been about five years.

Humming, I connected the hose to the stripped bed, threw the end out the window, and after a few minutes the mattress sagged into a fat mound of wrinkles.

Efficiently I reeled in the hose, walked it to the bathroom down the hall, and attached it to the faucet. Cold, clean water flowed back into the collapsed vinyl; in about twenty minutes, I'd have a fresh bed.

A few minutes later, the phone rang downstairs. My sister in California babbled a frightening story. She'd been making lunch in their ranch kitchen in the hills just outside Santa Barbara, when an odd movement caught her eye. A huge rattlesnake was crawling cautiously over the stone floor about seven feet away! The front door was open, and it had slithered through. Horrified, she screamed, causing her husband, who was writing a business report on the veranda, to rush in. He grasped the situation instantly. "Get up on the counter, then don't move! I'll be right back!" "Dee," she said, tearfully, "I've never moved so fast in my life. I flew up there, and it watched me! It watched me! Thirty minutes later I'm still finding it hard to breathe. Robin came back in with a shovel and chopped the snake's head off, but the fangs kept reflexively biting air; the mess in here is incredible. My legs wouldn't work; Robin had to help me down. If the kids had been here..." She began to cry.

Trying to calm her, I spoke soothingly. After a while, my daughter Jenny appeared around the corner, looking anxious.

"Mom," she said, tentatively, "um, the waterbed..."

I froze. Terror nearly overwhelmed me. Water... bed... maybe sixty minutes gone, and counting...

Screaming, I dropped the phone, pushed past Jenny, and shot up the stairs into a nightmare. The tortured, seam-stretched, bulging mattress LOOMED above me, an immense balloon trying to touch the ceiling. The old floor creaked under the enormous weight. Panting with fright I flew to the bathroom, shut off the faucet, detached the hose, rushed the nozzle to the bedroom window and began releasing the water. The kitchen, underneath, was seconds from disaster; our 150-year old brick farmhouse was sturdy, but this was surely too much.

Draining that bed was an agonizingly slow process. Time was a snail. I didn't breathe for twenty minutes.

Meanwhile, my sister dangled; the phone squawked distantly downstairs while I stared, hypnotized, at the monster. Any second the floor would collapse—any second...

Finally, a lifetime later, I inched delicately past the sagging, exhausted mattress, softly, softly crept downstairs to the phone, and spoke in a whisper, certain ANY vibration—any disturbance at all— would bring the house down. My frantic sister's relief was tremendous; I'd explained just enough before dropping the phone for her to piece together what had probably happened. Together we cried, and laughed, realizing how lucky we both were. I trembled for hours.

That afternoon, impossibly, an inspector pronounced the floor sound.

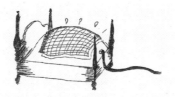

Resurrection of the Almost-Dead

YESTERDAY I WOKE UP LOWER than a snake's bottom. Sometimes this depressing environment—unfinished rooms cluttered with wires, pipes, paint cans, tarpaulins, scaffolding, not to mention my own dirty self—the sheer scale of the mess I've been trying to fix nearly undoes me. Rising was really difficult. Nothing helped. Not coffee, not lovely music from the painter's spattered CD player, not even my plane ticket hanging prominently on the kitchen wall, sporting a dumb silver bow.

I hate it when I find myself in the Pit of Despair.

Leaving four cleaners to tackle the wretched sunroom, I motored bleakly to Ross-on-Wye to shop for essentials, yet again. The sky looked threatening, the car demanded petrol, and my backpack chafed my shoulders. A black cloud hung over me as I walked Ross's very steep High Street (every British town's main street has that name). For tuppence I would have gone home to Joe. Right then.

Muttering about depressed old ladies muttering, I bought my ten thousandth cooked chicken, some sugar snap peas to munch, and, wincing, a liquid cleaner, Mr. Muscle. In America I won't eat anything or use any product that introduces itself as "Mr." (Mr. Hot Dog always got my goat.) But now I have no choice. The British stopped offering scouring powders like Comet years ago. Now there are only these inadequate spray cleaners.

They don't have Kraft Salad Dressing either. I long for a sandwich shmeered with that stuff...moan...

The British don't do sturdy wooden-handled straw brooms, either. Ever. Just darling, delicate little nylon push brooms in pretty colors that don't sweep and haven't a clue about cracks. No generously sized metal dustpans, either, just teeny pastel plastic ones that break. Their working life in my cottage is about one day. This dear little blue pan (number eight and counting) was tossed wearily into my basket. Poor thing. Its life was now measured in hours.

I paid, visited David, banked, scarfed down fish'n'chips, thumped to the car and motored home.

I nearly fell into the house jerking the heavy sliding door, as usual. That was the first clue. With a cleaned track now, it glided effortlessly. Then I sniffed CLEAN! The transformation was stunning. The long row of windows sparkled. The walls and ceiling had been scrubbed. The upholstered furniture, parked outside in fresh air, had been whacked with industrial strength rug beaters, then thoroughly vacuumed, then shampooed. On the polished dining table was my favorite green cloth, and, in a chipped mug, daffodils from Helen's Wood. The once-filthy curtains, washed yesterday by these cleaners, now hung happily. That venerable tweed carpet looked familiar: heavens, I'd forgotten its true color!

And then, the sun came out, making everything honey-gold.

Speechless, I bawled.

For four months I'd crawled over piles of boxes, coughed and gasped in that unlit pit, fallen many times because I'd lost my footing trying to navigate around endless power cables in the narrow track between mountainous piles. And now, ahhhh…now, I had a home again. Suddenly, I was back on track.

The cleaners proudly carried in the revived furniture; grinning, we arranged things. After giving the room a quick spray of freshener, they went home to clean themselves. They'd micro-scrubbed for seven hours, and changed the foul water in their huge machine five times. They were exhausted.

It was a resurrection for the sunroom, and for me. Though there is still much to do, this transformation turned me around.

I know now that I can do this, right to the end.

Senior Moments, Quacks, and The Donald

CLUTCHING MY LIST OF ERRANDS, I left Sunnybank's front door and meandered along Sixth Street, noting snoozing mallard pairs on the neighbors' lush, green, sunlit lawns. Grinning, I quacked quietly at their indifferent backs, then gleefully recalled a fascinating factoid. Donald Duck comics are banned in Finland—because he doesn't wear pants! As I thought this over, I nearly died laughing, having stepped into traffic after looking dutifully the wrong way. It was a close call. The horrified driver stood on his brakes and shouted "Are you nuts?!" while I stood there gaping. Idiot! I'd come safely home to the U.S., only to be nearly flattened by a two-ton car while giggling about Donald Duck running afowl of Finnish political quacks.

That near-hit got my attention. I made two resolutions: (1) When walking, I'll focus on American traffic patterns. (2) Silly thoughts of pantsless ducks will be (temporarily) banned.

Speaking of cars and confusion, I've just remembered a curious incident.

One morning an electrician rewiring our cottage in England had to pop out for a part, but my car blocked his. "I'll move it for you," he said. That suited me, as I was paint-spattered and high on a ladder. He got in, turned the key, then actually broke into a sweat when he discovered it wasn't a stick shift. The car jerked and hopped as his left foot pumped the brake, and his right foot pressed the accelerator while he shifted fruitlessly from drive to reverse. It was too much. Exiting hastily, he returned the key. "You do it. I could never drive one of those. I'd ruin it, or get distracted and cause an accident. Automatics are too confusing." (The vast majority of cars in Britain are stick shift models.) I was amazed.

Anyway, while I reorient, which takes a day or two, friends have driven me to appointments. Yesterday I walked all the way home from the dentist's office, from up M22. I found sixty-two cents on the sidewalk and admired Traverse Bay's elegant swans and noisy diving ducks (all without clothes), while subliminally relearning American traffic patterns.

Passing Tom's Market, I popped in to purchase a cinnamon roll. In the parking lot I noticed a mother and grandmother trying to round up four small, rambunctious children to be strapped into their car seats. Mountains of folded clothes sat in stacked plastic laundry baskets, which were squeezed into their car. Seeing me, gran looked startled, then grinned. "Oh, I remember you; you were thee topic at dinner two months ago. Where do you get your ideas?" I thanked her happily, visibly puffing up, while mentally reviewing my columns. Which one...? Expertly snatching another youngster, she went on.

"I watched you again the other day. You're really clever, you know, pulling tons of laundry through snow and ice to your car without breaking a sweat, using bungee cords to connect your three baskets. Inspiring! That idea changed how my daughter and I manage laundry. I've got four grandkids, you know, including triplets. My washer collapsed ages ago, along with my back. Now, leaving the laundromat for the car, we just hitch four baskets together, settle the kids in with the folded clothes, and 'pull the train.' Easy as pie! Thanks!"

Waving, they drove off, honking.

Staring after them I downed the last bit of roll, and licked my fingers thoughtfully. Not a bad idea, that laundry-basket bit. But it wasn't me they'd seen.

Walking along, I reflected that Donald doesn't duck helping his mischievous nephews, triplets Huey, Dewey, and Louie. But he never does the laundry. His life is simpler.

Finally, featherheaded Finns have forgotten that, when he swims, Donald Fauntleroy Duck always wears a suit.

Diligent Dilbert Delivers: Part One

BACK IN AMERICA, I BEGAN to write another column, then realized that it would be about England again. I simply haven't been back here long enough to collect and narrate events, memories, and feelings about my life here. Honestly, I'm still reeling from my four-month British cottage adventure.

The other night I woke, shouting, from a nightmare about rats. I'd fought large ones for a long time. Shocked by England's record-breaking snowy winter these forest rodents, driven by hunger and cold, had boldly moved into the ruined cottage.

Nightly I retreated to the cottage's blessedly intact back bedroom, usually as soon as it got too dark to see—about 6:00 P.M.—and fell thankfully into bed. My hot water bottle saved me from freezing. It was heavenly to snuggle down with four layers of clothes on, hugging it. Though I heard noises while drifting into a deep sleep, I shrugged them off. But as the days passed, and I tried to salvage what wasn't flood-ravaged, I began to realize the cottage was infested. As I cleaned I saw rats running along the walls from the corner of my eye. And I heard them. (Rats make high, unpleasant raspy squeak-shrieks.)

I laid down poison, and three days later I noticed bodies. Once, while I was chatting with a workman in the ruined library, a dead rat clunked down onto my shoulder from out of the collapsed ceiling. The workmen were horrified. I was delighted. Soon, bodies littered the house and garden. For a few days, having heard and seen nothing, I felt smug. Gotcha!

Then, the second wave hit. One terrible midnight found them gnawing, gnawing, gnawing through the wall between the bathroom and bedroom. Those sounds were magnified, out there in the forest. Wall-banging helped, for about an hour. I woke again to find three running across the bed. I leaped out, switched on the big torch, and yelled, angrily; alarmed, the creatures vanished through the hole they'd made. Furious, I covered it with a heavy bag of worksite nails. Those rats had met their match!
Time for the big guns.

Furious, I rang a friend who keeps horses. She recommended her rat man. "He'll sort you. Dilbert lives to kill rats."

The guy, hearing my desperation, came immediately. A tall, eager, whippet-slim man in his mid-sixties with tufts of clean white hair that stood straight up, he was dressed tidily in cords, with a pressed shirt and a warm vest. "Don't ye worry, lassie—I'll get 'em. Nary a tail will ye see..."

He hugged me, grinned, then cheerfully began the hunt. That elderly man scoured every foot of ground within seventy feet of the house, climbed up to the roof, searched the eaves, explored the exterior stone walls, and investigated every indoor inch. Occasionally I'd hear a delighted yelp, or a chuckle, sprinkled with "tsks."

Finally, we toured. Rats had simply stepped from the drooping branches of the huge cedars onto the roof, then entered through cracks, which they'd enlarged with their sharp claws and incisors. They'd tunneled under the foundations, and come up through the floors. Dilbert showed me where the earth was packed down; feces and bits of half-munched birdseed were beacons to this dedicated hunter.

From his car he removed six black plastic briefcases housing industrial-strength poison that kills, leaving no odor. These were strategically placed at well-traveled entrances. He plugged interior rat holes with tightly wadded newspapers. "If these are shifted, it tells me they're still coming." He paused, then added, quietly, "But the papers won't move." His eyes twinkled. "They're done for, lassie."

What happened then? Tune in next Sunday.

Diligent Dilbert Delivers: Part Two

RATS HAD OVERWHELMED OUR flood-ruined, single story cottage in England; after battling them unsuccessfully for three weeks, I hired a professional, Dilbert, who'd dispatched rats for forty-five years. His wife cheerfully announced he had a one-hundred-percent success rate. Perfect! After scrutinizing the terrain, he strategically placed multiple black plastic rat-boxes in and out of the cottage, with inviting, rat-sized entrances. Their interiors held delectable, fatal niblets. *Rattus rattus* would dine, lick his lips happily, then painlessly expire, usually in three or four days.

Dilbert loved his work, and, eyes shining, he tackled this job with enthusiasm. It was a true rescue. I was desperate, exhausted, and needed a champion. Dilbert was a modern knight.

But now, having laid the traps, he sighed. "Now, lassie, this poison works wonders—slowly. Lodge in Ross-on-Wye a wee while—four days. You shouldn't sleep here just now."

I resisted. No rodent would evict me!

That day my friend Aaron and I decided to clean the attic. He opened the ceiling trapdoor, lowered the ladder, and ascended. I was about to follow, but then, suddenly, he stiffened, backed hastily down the ladder, and feverishly re-secured the door. A dozen large, red-eyed rats had formed a ragged circle up there, and glared at him, whiskers twitching. Aaron is a farm lad, and I've never seen him quail, but now he turned to me, upset. "Get out of here tonight, Dee. These rats consider us invaders. Females are protecting their nests; I think Dilbert's right."

Healthy forests are full of animals, including rodents, and we lived nearly surrounded by a lovely wood. Rats are clever, social, and quick to take advantage of a situation like mine. Normally shy and nonconfrontational, they were now in protection mode.

I went into my sanctuary to make the bed, and froze. The walls were alive! Loud gnawing sounds radiated from new places, along with occasional, muffled squeaks. I realized that tonight could be very bad, indeed. I'd be stupid to stay here. There are times to hold the line, and times to fold up one's tent and retreat.

I motored to the ancient, beautiful Royal Hotel in Ross-on-Wye. A tiny, snug room became my home, for a token fee. The management knew my story, as I would sometimes eat a meal there and chat with them. That first night I showered for ages, savoring the hot water, then fell into bed, sleeping twelve hours. Breakfast, included, was luxury; for the first time in eons, I feasted.

Fortified, I motored home. Workmen and I ripped down ceilings, steamed off rotting wallpaper, sanded, and applied full-strength bleach to moldy walls. Rat nests and droppings were everywhere. I found my mother's high school diploma chewed to shreds; its Latin decree lined a nest.

On the third day bodies began turning up, between tools, amid bags of lime and plaster, and under fresh-cut replacement timber. I moved back the fifth night, to perfect quiet. Subsequent visits by the triumphant rat man confirmed it: my tattered home was reclaimed.

A week before I left, an amazed workman yelled and sat back from securing a cover over an electrical wall socket: huge, languorous flies were emerging from these wire-crammed holes. We were fascinated. Finally, Aaron solved the mystery.

Rats had died in the walls, blowflies immediately laid eggs, and mature flies were now emerging. Disgusting, but true. Dilbert confirmed that, though there was no smell, a few rats had expired in there. The situation would resolve eventually.

The cottage, rat-free, is lovely now, but I will never forget that battle for territory. Proper Trojan horses, full of lethal weaponry, used intelligently, had dispatched a most determined enemy.

Dilbert visits once monthly, to make sure.

It's a Wonderful Life!

I WAS SCARFING DOWN a delicious shepherd's pie at the Ax and Cleaver pub in the English village of Much Birch, where our family cottage was being restored after a devastating flood. A tiny neatly-dressed old lady sat down at the next table; I saw her reading a Miss Read book, and we struck up a conversation.

Millicent, seventy-two years old, was a widow. Ten years before, her husband, a minister, had died suddenly, leaving her alone in a drafty parsonage in Essex. One morning shortly thereafter, she calculated that she had spent forty-six years in her kitchen, willingly preparing tasty meals for village fêtes and a myriad of other good causes.

Suddenly, the thought of preparing one more such meal seemed intolerable. Shocked by this revelation, she'd grown thoughtful, then resolute. Pulling out a suitcase, she'd packed her Bible, a map, some sturdy clothes, two pairs of shoes, and a serviceable coat, and set out to see the (English) world. The woman was a true nomad. She simply went wherever, staying a day, or weeks. Sometimes, she admitted wryly, she'd let her faithful Ford Escort choose. Evenings were spent reading and charting the past week's route. Her frayed map was a linear diary of where she'd been over the years. Lines crossed and re-crossed. Some villages had red stars; residents there had become friends.

"I'd never left the village where I'd been born, my dear, so, with no reason not to, I decided to live an opposite life. Each day is a surprise." She grinned. "I haven't prepared a meal in over a decade. I've a reasonable pension, and possess an ATM card. B and Bs are usually run by interesting older ladies, so I'm seldom lonely. And, I like shocking them silly with my lifestyle. They sometimes look at me with secret longing; I think their tethers get wearying, at times.

"I do keep certain rules, such as never driving at night, arriving well before dark so I can choose a reasonable hotel or B and B, and avoiding cities. They're too nerve-racking.

I use charity shops to vary my outfits; those places have clean, serviceable clothes. I enjoy getting my hair done, though sometimes the color is blue." She sighed, happily. "Blue, white, grey, I don't honestly care. I just want easy, and respectable.

"I know where the best cream teas are served, where to find lovely country gardens, and how to avoid officious, snooty self-important women directing tourists through enormous rooms in drafty castles stuffed with vacant armor, Roman busts, and gigantic portraits of more snooty aristocrats. Lunchrooms in these piles serve dismal sandwiches and weak tea. But I love wandering their grounds, imagining intriguing lives lived so long ago."

She sighed again, content. "It's a wonderful life! I hope I can go on for a few more years. After that I'll choose a room by the sea, in a comfy boarding house, perhaps near friends I've made, and settle in. God will decide the rest. I do enjoy making my way through the adventures of Miss Read, an English spinster school teacher in a village so like mine; I've at least twenty-two more books to look forward to." Popping in a frayed bookmark, she closed the latest one.

Dabbing her lips she rose, smiled and shook my hand firmly. "I'm off! I've enjoyed our chat."

She paused. "I suppose my unconventional life seems unthinkable to you, but I've never felt so alive. England is truly a green and pleasant land. I do feel such a part of it. Goodbye."

A sign in her car's back window read: "Variety Is The Spice Of Life."

Who could disagree?

A Fair Day in Herefordshire

WHAT A FUNNY WORLD. ON Thursday morning I was rooting around in my beloved Traverse City garden, and on Friday Joe and I were whizzing through the English countryside toward our cottage. Roads gleamed in a misty rain; rabbits, oddly golden in the Friday evening light, darted brainlessly in front of our taxi.

This ten-day return trip was necessary. The insurance claim wants settling. We'll visit David (my late mother's cherished husband), now happily snug in a lovely countryside care home nearby. He's felt much safer there, surrounded by devoted caregivers. Finally, we'll simply enjoy the cottage I'd spent the first four months of 2009 renovating, after a Christmas flood nearly destroyed it.

Dilbert, the rat man, had coincidentally just arrived for his regular inspection. Cheerful, confident there'd be not a trace of the buck-toothed bad guys, he made his careful rounds while colorfully narrating to Joe how I'd battled those monsters. I preened, and fluffed my fur, modestly. (Of course, you'd be right to mutter into your sleeve that only an idiot would wait three weeks to call for help, instead choosing to shoot, poison, and try to intimidate Rattus rattus. Finally, outnumbered and surrounded, I'd prudently practiced strategic retreat while Dilbert the Terminator did it right.)

Copious English rain has encouraged the thistles in Helen's Wood to shoot up eight feet, but the cottage area is lovely, thanks to our care-taker's efforts. Exuberant nasturtiums tumble over the main walk's stone walls, while the raised garden hosts gorgeous red-hot pokers, lush sedums, and honey-gold daylilies.

On Sunday, the annual Herefordshire Country Fair beckoned. We motored down wafer-narrow, centuries-old hedge-lined lanes, until long car lines in the middle of nowhere indicated we'd arrived. (Two cars traveling the opposite way made endless autos "hedge-hug"; curious sheep enjoyed the steel ballet as the hapless motorists only just squeezed past. Baa!)

The vast field was filled with fascinating craft booths, food tents, sheepdog competitions and kiddie rides. And dogs. Families wandered about, accompanied by long, hairy lurchers; eager beagles; enigmatic Australian ridgebacks; keen Jack Russell terriers and devoted black-and-white border collies. Everywhere you looked, there were dogs the size of ponies; you would think they'd all be fighting. But even when they were paired on loose double leashes, the canine multitudes never misbehaved.

Strollered infants bumped along, waving colorful, handcrafted toys. Balloons bobbled, and doggied adults jovially exchanged local gossip. One tent housed bored, rescued owls; a giant red sign—STOLEN TOOL COMPANY—trumpeted somebody's business. A salmon fisherman demonstrating technique in the tumbling river bisecting the fair had devotees watching every move from a roped off, respect-ful distance.

Beautiful ponies, with immaculately togged children aboard, waited their turns to competitively jump small fences. Announcers blared scores and encouraged applause.

Corralled baby llamas munched food, donkeys brayed, soulful res-cued greyhounds hoped for adoption, leashed falcons squawked, and a helicopter bearing parents and saucer-eyed children roared off; each thrilling ride lasted seven minutes.

Then I gasped! Perched jauntily atop a hay bale gleamed a pair of narrow-heeled, electric green Wellington boots! I'd never seen any-thing like them. They beckoned me; I swooned. Just fifteen pounds, and—oh, joy, they fit! SOLD. Cramming soiled sneakers into my backpack, I wellied gleefully down the muddy, manured midway. I was impossible to ignore. Joe couldn't stop laughing; I grinned till my cheeks ached.

One guy sold hot dogs. In Britain? Fascinated, we bought one, heaped it with ketchup and slithery cooked onions, gobbled it down, and licked our fingers. Yum!

Contented, we finally staggered home. Farm-made ice cream smudges and bits of straw and earth decorated rumpled our trousers and sleeves. Perfumed evening air soothed two tired country mice into sleep.

Another Dumb Bunny Bummer

SOMETIMES I LOOK FOR ME everywhere. My hare-brained thoughts keep me in contention for the Dumb Bunny of the Month award. Read on.

I was invited to Mensa's July luncheon meeting at a Traverse City restaurant to rattle on about my column (especially the "England saga") and mingle with the folks. To quote Google: "Mensa, an international society, has only one requirement for membership—a score in the top two percent on a standardized IQ test. It's not political, and holds no opinions, but serves as a social organization, and promotes research in the area of human intelligence." This lunch would be really interesting.

I laid out some nice clothes so as to make a good impression. (I clean up pretty well, but it's a struggle.)

After it had been in my date book for nearly five months, the big day came. I got the garden chores done, and, humming, collected all my tools...and then I saw the algae. It sat by the pool, on a wet brick, looking particularly beguiling, dressed in lovely colors— gray-green with blue flecks, along with a splash of orangey-brown. It hosted interesting bugs. Hands-and-knees time. A ladybug was a ruby atop the algae; an earwig wandered underneath the brick; ants, ignoring it, marched out of a hole next door, busy with their own agendas. I admired the formidable pincers on the earwig's rear end, and wondered how it must feel to drag that equipment around one's whole life. How did it manage to mate? Ouch...

It doesn't take a Mensa member to see where this is going.

I got lost. As surely as a bat with its radar down. Knees-in-grass, I conjured up silly scenarios, imagining the armed earwig waging backside battles with pill bugs, ants and the odd microorganism. Hmmm...Could algae learn to display colors when sensing destructive feet, mimicking annoyed octopuses (octopi?)? Meanwhile, visitors came and went. Time passed. I dreamed.

Knowing I fall into mental rabbit holes at awkward times, I've made rules. Here's one: Never "disappear" while cooking. Why? Bored with sautéing a chicken's thigh this past June, I'd mentally wandered off: Would a major eruption of the Cumbre Vieja volcano in the Canary Islands trigger a monumental landslide that would trigger a mega-tsunami that would overwhelm America's Eastern seaboard?

The neglected chicken charred. The fire alarm squawked, triggering a call from Minneapolis alarm headquarters. Only then did I finally notice smoke and hurtle back.

Groan...Obviously, I hadn't learned from this embarrassment.

Bug-watching was interrupted when my neglected stomach finally growled. I trotted reluctantly into the house to sniff around for food, and realized there wasn't any. Huh. How could I have forgotten to visit the grocery? Then, BANG! I was rocked! Nooooo... To say I was horrified is to barely graze the surface of my chagrin. Lost in space, I'd forgotten the lunch I'd anticipated for weeks.

Flame-cheeked, I reassembled myself just enough to ring the

restaurant. The club's chairman came on—by then, everyone was leaving—and I fervently apologized, saying I'd gotten distracted by garden events. But it was an edited truth. How could I explain what had really happened—that I'd tripped out on algae? How would that go over?

He was incredibly gracious, which this dummy, feeling like slime mold, certainly didn't deserve. I'd flunked the test that really mattered.

What's that sage observation? "One is judged by the company one keeps." But schmoozing with brain-dead algae, for heaven's sake?

Telling, eh?

A Car-Chosen, Timeless Tour

ONE ENGLISH MORNING IN AUGUST, Joe and I decided to let our little car choose which country lanes to explore. Idle nearly three months, and bored (as I'd returned to T.C. in mid-May), this suited it perfectly. Off we went, the GPS lady's voice content to simply note our course through the lovely rural parts of Herefordshire. (When we'd had enough, we'd simply press "home"; she'd "consult the stars" and unerringly guide us back.)

We popped into bustling Hereford to milk a cash point (ATM machine). Then, after a quick look around, the car's bonnet pointed roughly north (British cars wear bonnets and boots, you know) and we were off!

The day was fine. Falcons and buzzards soared high, their keen eyes scanning the lush, endless hills and valleys for silly mice out for a frolic. The sun shone kindly on this massive, gorgeous panorama. Climbing high we chugged along, windows down, wishing the English believed in scenic overview stops. Never mind: no one was behind us, so we moved slowly, savoring some of the finest rural landscape in the world.

Oh! For a few seconds, achingly lovely, mysterious perfection flashed by...

Close your eyes. Picture a long, slim, paved country lane framed either side by precisely planted, half-century old oaks that emphasize its gentle curve to the vanishing point. Sunlight filters benignly through those sentinels' lush leaves onto a closely mown carpet of dappled, emerald grass...

That fleeting image will remain with me always.

Twelve miles and over half an hour later, a small, weathered sign (nearly smothered by a determined hedge) struggled to announce the way to Weobley (pronounced WEB-ley). Weobley, the sign said, was voted the most beautiful black-and-white half-timbered village in England in 1996.

Hmmm. Joe and I love England's cherished, ancient architecture. (Hereford, population seventy thousand, has wonderful examples.) Deciding, the car ambled slowly down toward Weobley's heart. A few bends and tall hedges later, there it was. Ancient cottages, pleasingly slanted under the weight of centuries, framed the lovely central village commons. Several incredibly old, gently off-center shops next to them sold books, kitchen implements and gardening supplies. A church steeple pierced the white-fleeced blue sky; sheep grazed peacefully across from its cemetery. You could put Weobley (population seven hundred) in your pocket.

The sun blessed profusely flowering baskets and geraniumed windowsills, but, aside from a parked car or two in its tree-framed, light-drenched center, there was no sign of life. No people, even in high summer. Not even cats or dogs...We'd stepped straight into a postcard. My skin prickled.

Time hesitated, stopped. We looked. And looked.

Across the commons a skirted grey-haired lady left her little cottage to visit the nearby Royal Post Office. She paused. Our eyes met.

Looking around contentedly she nodded, then smiled, knowing all about enchantment.

An eight-hundred-year old pub overlooking the market square served solid English fare. Three locals sipping lager acknowledged us, then continued conversing in low murmurs. Two tasty Ploughman's Lunches later we emerged, blinking, to walk slowly to Weobley's fourteenth-century church.

Its cool, dim interior boasted vaulted ceilings and stained glass windows. Protruding from huge stone pillars were ten half-size beardless medieval men's heads, smiling, looking disgruntled, puzzled, annoyed or amused. One was outright laughing! They delighted me. Rich perfume emanated from freshly cut lilies; graves with their residents' likenesses commemorated in marble were sprinkled throughout. It was dead quiet.

Car and guide got us home; still bewitched, we hardly noticed. For one brief, shining moment, the mental flu so prevalent these days—madding crowds, and a myriad of modern worries—had, with a dose of rural England's timeless elixir, vanished.

Bumping Heads with British Bankers

A smooth sea never made a skillful mariner. —English proverb

IT'S INCREDIBLY FRUSTRATING TO FUNCTION financially in England if one lacks British citizenship. Even dangling deposit money in front of official noses doesn't dent their demeanor.

"Good morning, sir. Your utility company is deducting 215 pounds monthly for propane gas, but as our cottage, in the midst of flood-restoration, hasn't used gas for eight months, this seems excessive" (I've mastered the British art of understatement). "Further, you keep insisting Mr. Firks wasn't born on his birthday. May we discuss it?"

"Certainly, madam. May I have your account number?...Thank you. Are you Mrs. Firks? No? Clearly, you are not Mr. Firks, either. Unfortunately, we" (note the imperial "we"!) "cannot review this matter with anyone but him. And since you are not listed on this account, we are powerless to continue."

"But," I protested, "I merely want to discuss these charges."

"Alas," he pontificated unctuously, "though you are a relation, you are not the account holder, so further discussion is impossible." I was cheerfully wished a good day. Click.

(Power-of-attorney papers are in the works; meanwhile, these outrageous fees continue to be deducted.)

I couldn't open even a savings account there. Executive eyes became hooded, postures stiffened, and officials developed long-distance looks as they moved into computer mode. "We are sorry, but it is not possible to accommodate your request. You are not British."

"But," I protested, "I merely want to insert funds INTO your bank for the purpose of paying monthly bills."

"We are sorry," they chorused, "but this is not possible."

I developed calluses on my forehead from banging it on British bank walls. Every august institution viewed me as a potential terrorist. Though I patiently explained my situation at Bryn Garth Cottage— how I needed to transfer U.S. funds to pay bills and finance restoration until the insurance claim was settled—it didn't matter two pins. Rules Were Rules. "Aliens may not open an account," one starched-undies banker sniffed—"money-laundering, you know." Though I protested I'd never laundered more than my dirty clothes, he wouldn't budge. Bureaucracy and I— Elephant and gnat— bumped noses. I got stomped flat.

Baffled, I retreated into a teashop to rethink things. Problems have solutions. What I needed was a banker able to think outside the box. Uh-huh. That sort is scarcer than a vampire craving yogurt.

My solution? A British offshore bank. Back in the U.S., I filled out a zillion forms, but no matter how many gold-sealed, notarized documents were sent from my accountant, banker, lawyer, etc., they weren't satisfied. When another letter arrived, declaring they needed more proof I was harmless—proof not required in the previous letter—I blew.

With massive self-control I rang them and quietly announced they'd changed the rules in the middle of the game. I wouldn't provide One. More. Scrap. of paper. They'd either approve me, or send back my three-thousand-pound deposit immediately.

Hmmm. He thought it over. Bankers hate money going out. "I'll ring you back, madam."

"Fine," said I. "You have two hours. Decide."

Five minutes before the deadline he rang. They were delighted to welcome me into their bank.

(Ha! I allowed myself a fist in the air!) Briskly, staying passionless, I requested checkbook and debit card immediately. They roared through the post in four days.
That's power.

Now I pay bills in pounds sterling without paying English lawyers to pay them, and save the forty-five dollars incurred every time I'd wire money.

As always, adversity is simply opportunity in work clothes.

Battling a Slow-Motion Monster

ENGLAND HAS A SIMPLY GLORIOUS climate. Herefordshire's growing season lasts ten months a year. Believe it.

But monsters lurk in this paradise. A laurel hedge lives on my property. "So?" you say. "Sounds innocuous enough." Uh-huh...so are charming, conscience-less sociopaths, initially. They smile winningly, and are masters of socially correct behavior. They seem eager to please, and are easy on the eye.

English laurel hedges are like that.

But let's start at the beginning.

When Mother and David moved in 1981 from the Isle of Skye to Bryn Garth Cottage in England, they wanted to muffle the traffic sounds coming from the two-lane highway far below. Laurel introduced itself at a local nursery. It sat in its pot, those fat, perfect leaves thick, shiny and unblemished, ignored by disease or insects. The nursery assistant assured them it would provide rapid coverage. The shrub fluffed its leaves and smiled its best; they were charmed. Ten plump

hedgelings were escorted home and planted at the bottom of the garden, which was drenched in sunshine and the red, iron-rich soil for
which Herefordshire is so justly famous.

For a few years all was well. Annual trims kept it tidy.

But this plant had an uncomplicated plan. Simply stated, it aimed for
world domination. It went about this goal stealthily, always careful
to stay green and lush. Wrist-thick stumps filled out within weeks
of being trimmed—the first hint of trouble. But this subtle clue was
missed.

Anchored now on the edge of the steep hillside by huge, thigh-thick
roots, it began to move inexorably toward the house. Mother had
established a glorious flower garden within its borders, but every year
she noticed her beds seemed—well, smaller than last year... but that
was silly.

The laurel moved closer. One night, while a soft English rain fell, this
monster, quietly munching mineral-rich soil, assessed the situation.
Established now, it had sun, space, food, and nobody was watching. GO!

Practically overnight, it's overrun everything. It's fallen backward to
race fifty feet down the steep hill. It's flopped forward, the bottom
branches curving into an "L" to reach for the sky. It's shot straight
up, thickly green, rapidly reaching thirty feet high. When howling
gale-force winds from the Welsh mountains roar over the landscape,
the laurel doesn't flinch. It's snacked on the century-old, thick stone
wall bordering the cottage, smothered young trees and surrounded
giant oaks. And it's squeezed the long asphalt driveway smaller and
smaller...

Finally, far too late, Mother and David grasped the situation. The
garden was ten feet narrower. Desperately they hired a team of men to

chainsaw the hedge to five feet high; it took three days, cost a fortune, and made no difference, as six months later it had to be done again. The hedge was fifty feet wide now, impenetrable, and relentlessly expanding in every direction.

Somehow it's found a way to enter the forest to one side of the cottage. There, a twiglet has grown into a gigantic, thirty-foot high/wide towering menace, overwhelming everything. Laurel is everywhere.

Then Mother died. David moved to a residential care home. I was left to gape at the incredible power of this beautiful monster.

I've hired a ruthless team of burly men and their huge digger/ripper machine to extract just the lawn hedge, in October. This dangerous, exhausting work will cost thousands of pounds, and take two weeks. As for the forest growth, control is illusory. But I'm absolutely determined. This hedge has met its match!

English workmen look at me under their helmets, and shake their heads. They know better…

The Beginning of the End

AWK! IT'S A MADHOUSE AROUND HERE! All the furniture has just been redelivered after having been in storage for two months. Men and equipment are everywhere. I've just stepped on Sparky, the prone electrician (who yelped, then grinned), and squeezed past the long-suffering painter. I pull up sofa cushions to expose a rat's birdseed stash, crammed between them. (That discovery reminded me how fiercely I'd battled those huge, determined home invaders, for over three months.) Today, six days before I return to America, is the busiest since this saga began. The end of four months of hard work is at hand.

The "removals" van (a lorry long as Manhattan) is parked in the driveway's wide apron; two burly men grimace and puff as they haul endless boxes of books up thirty big stairs, through the front door. More furniture and boxed dishes follow. Paraphernalia are plunked down in the rooms they'll be folded into. Walkways narrow to toothpick-thin. My visiting sister Kath and our cousin Nancy unwrap each beautifully packed item; shouts of delighted recognition ring through the din. "Hey, I remember when Mom/Aunt Barb bought this..." Mountainous discarded paper soon envelops both ladies; comments become muffled. I desperately cram wads back into emptied containers and shove them out the door. Soon that's blocked. Huge, languorous black flies buzz about, and overweight bumblebees, bewildered by walls and windows, hover, confused, over flowery dishes. (The British don't do screens, ever.) Bryn Garth cottage is bursting at the seams with boxes, bodies and bonhomie.

Two desperate carpet fitters, who have removed the pantry toilet's door, try to measure and cut as bodies tramp past. Shouts of "The bloody loo door is gone and we need a toilet!" distract me from gathering paper. I open the master bathroom to the relieved workers. Soon a ragged, chatty queue forms.

One carpenter's saw whines just outside the cottage; both "chippies" fashion waist-high library wall panels that look posh, but are made quick and cheap.

Three gardeners on the nearby patio pry out Godzilla-sized dandelions from the fountain's rim. (Weeds here rocket to mammoth proportions in Britain's ten-month growing season.)

Three cleaners climb ladders to avoid being trampled while they wipe down each filthy, ceiling-high bookshelf. Soon they'll unpack, wipe clean, and place each tome in its home. Steadily, foot by foot, that lovely room emerges. I need only poke my head in there to feel my spirits soar.

The plumber, carrying a radiator, inches past boxes and bodies until, finally losing patience, he mutters that he'll return tomorrow when the madness subsides and he can actually move well enough to do his job. Gulp. I sense his frustration is huge. As he leaves, I contemplate begging...my bathroom is freezing. But I stifle myself, cultivate a stiff upper lip and resign myself, with a sigh, to one more cold night.

Toward day's end, working flat out, things are nearly sorted. Finishing touches will happen for the next three days, then...heavens. It's difficult to grasp, but I think I might have a decent, done home, here.

Kath, Nancy and I open a dusty bottle of Spanish wine, then slice
Double Gloucester cheese and crusty bread to dip in olive oil and salt;
after months of paper plates, real dishes clatter. The sun flames out
in a giant, fiery ball of brilliant orange behind the Black Mountains
as we survey the still-messy cottage with satisfaction. I run around
switching on lights and poking dust-free sofas, thrilled. Then, in
the soft English twilight, we toast a two-hundred-year old beauty
snatched back from the brink:

> To a lovely cottage:
> May misfortune follow you
> All the days of your life—
> And never again catch up!

Home is Where the Heart Is

HOME. SUCH A SMALL WORD to harbor such heartfelt meaning. Home, to familiar sniffs, to cheerful waiters offering endless cups of real coffee; home to everything I'd missed so keenly; home to Joe, to my life.

Funny—it's taking more time than I thought it would, to feel fully here in Traverse City. A good part of me is still in Herefordshire, in Bryn Garth cottage's lovely, breezy, window-lined sunroom, gazing down between clean, gossamer-white curtains upon Golden Valley's incomparable spring beauty. Perhaps it's taking so long to let go because I'd had just fifteen precious minutes to savor things, there. At 2:45 P.M., the last workman departed. The cottage preened, reborn. I'd wandered through the rooms memorizing the lines, the lightness of it all, the sense of completion. It had my stamp, and didn't mind. Nothing fought. Colors married with the natural light; books beckoned. The comfy library's upholstered chairs invited, rugs flopped happily on floors, and my mother's beautifully restored desk (pummeled by torrents of water for two weeks in December) rested in its place. Everything gleamed, as the cleaners had returned to pounce on lingering dust that morning. How enormously satisfying.

A fat, tiny, orange-breasted robin peered in the window, and velvet-furred rabbits played on the newly-mown lawn. I sat on the window seat marveling at this metamorphosis—from "shoulda plowed it under" to perfect.

Well, nearly. The guest bedroom was still unfinished. No worries—another two days would put it right. But now, with pictures and curtains hung, I hugged myself, and solemnly pronounced it Done.

Three o'clock. A car door slammed. My dear, long-time English friend had arrived to take me away. Bounding up the stone stairs she blew into the house, exclaiming at the order. We high-fived, I offed the lights, locked the door, and we were gone, leaving the cottage bewildered. Unexpectedly, I felt a searing wrench, then tears. How could I leave? This was abandonment!

"Wait! Take me back!" I wanted to scream! But on we motored to Newport's train connection. (Hereford was celebrating Mayfair, a huge annual seven-hundred-year-old festival that only an Act of Parliament can abolish, making it impossible to use that train station.) Gaynor chattered cheerfully about positive things. "Relax," she said. "It'll be fine..."

Abruptly Joe thumped down the stairs into Sunnybank's warm, suitcase-messy kitchen, wreathed in grins, arms open, shirttails out, shoeless feet slapping the pine floor. I leaped up, and into those welcoming arms. This is why I came back.

He said, straight away, knowing me so well, "We'll go back there regularly, you know. We can have feet in both worlds. Bryn Garth will be fine; good people are looking after it."

The phone rang; my children shouted a welcome. Best friends Les and Sarah grilled Delmonico steaks, and I inhaled her incredible cookies. Lovely music filled the house (except for the painter's offerings, there'd been none at Bryn Garth—no TV or newspaper either—for four months). The neighbor cat wound round the porch banister, fat with kittens. My garden gleamed, attentively cleaned by my friend Adam, of Timeless Gardens.

I looked at bright tulips, the fountains, the promise of it all, and felt a great welling of eagerness for the life I'd left so abruptly. Rolling my eyes, I snatched away the silly silk Christmas poinsettias from the porch wall vases, and swept the front walk with a Broom.

With an audible snap, I'd disengaged from over there, and was truly home.